IRISH RAILWAY
ALBUM

Ex Great Southern and Western Railway 4-6-0 (CIE class B2) No 409 being prepared for a Cork to Dublin freight working in 1955. This class was built in 1921 for the heaviest express passenger work on the Dublin-Cork main line, but were rapidly displaced in the later 1950s by the class A Metrovick diesels.

[R. Stieber

IRISH RAILWAY ALBUM

C. P. Boocock

LONDON

IAN ALLAN

7110   0043   3

Published in the United Kingdom by Ian Allan Ltd, Shepperton, Surrey, and printed by Crampton & Sons Ltd, Sawston, Cambridge.

Contents

All photographs are by the author unless otherwise indicated

Preface

IT IS FITTING to record in print and pictures the Irish railway scene now that steam traction has all but ceased to exist there. The author has made four happy visits to Ireland, in 1956, 1957, 1963 and 1967. This period has witnessed the most fundamental changes this century in the extent and operation of railways in Northern Ireland and Eire, and the photographs in this album illustrate many of the changes made.

In 1956 trains in different parts of Ireland could be seen with steam, diesel, electric and even horse traction. Now, diesel traction remains supreme. Three 3ft gauge lines still ran in 1959. The last of these closed in 1960. Of the five individually identifiable railways operating in 1957, closures and nationalisation have reduced them to the two undertakings now in control.

On several occasions the author was able to visit railway installations and to travel on some footplates. His thanks and acknowledgements are offered to the managements of CIE, UTA, GNRB, CDRJC, SL&NCR and the Guinness Brewery for the facilities and information that were so helpfully given.

Introduction

IT WAS IN 1956 that the author made his first acquaintance with the railways of Ireland. This divided country had a relaxed atmosphere unequalled in the author's experience anywhere in Western Europe this side of the Pyrénées.

In Eire particularly the railways reflected this easy-going quality. Their development over the years was a mirror of the country's fortunes. After the "troubles" in the 1920s, until when the railways' technical standards equalled good practice elsewhere in Britain, the railways of the Free State suffered a long period of financial starvation during which very few technical advances could be made, until the 1950s and 1960s. Then, along with the upsurge in industrial activity in Eire, a sudden and effective modernisation of the railways took place, with some pruning of unremunerative routes, culminating in the elimination of steam locomotives operated by the Republic's railways by 1963.

In Northern Ireland continued progress was made after the division of the country in maintaining the principal railways in an up-to-date condition. It is apparently odd therefore that some steam traction should still remain there at the time of writing, even if only in a minor role, after excessively severe closures had been completed throughout the area.

One effect of these events was to evolve a railway network that in the mid to late 1950s exhibited some staggering contrasts. For example, one could see a modern, diesel locomotive hauled train of new stock on a broad gauge express working from Dublin to Sligo leaving Dromod station, while simmering quietly at a platform nearby stood a 3ft gauge 2-4-2T (second hand from a defunct Cork suburban line) on a mixed train destined for Ballinamore, centre of the famed Cavan and Leitrim Railway. It was possible to hire from the post office at Ballinamore an aged bicycle, as did the author in 1957, and to cycle along the Drumshambo road alongside which ran that most Irish of all narrow gauge branches, the Arigna line: some good strong pedalling here enabled the author to take four successive photographs of a well laden coal train hauled graciously if slowly by a Tralee and Dingle 2-6-0T.

Where else but in Ireland could one travel in a six year old narrow gauge diesel railcar to find level crossing gates firmly shut in front of the car (twice) to be opened on the first occasion by a barefooted boy, and on the second by no-one until the guard climbed down to do so?

This is not to suggest that Irish railways were inefficient and unreliable. Not so. The author never missed a booked connection in Ireland during some 2,000 miles' travel there. On the Northern Counties section of the Ulster Transport Authority he footplated a Derby built 2-6-0 working at speed through well laid passing loops that permitted automatic tablet catching at 60 mph. On that smartly run railway, the Great Northern, where staff morale always seemed so high, he enjoyed travelling in heavy trains at speed behind the lovely blue Glover compound and McIntosh three cylinder simple 4-4-0s. And in the south, on the railways of Coras Iompair Eireann, lightweight coaches running on Commonwealth bogies had, by 1956, brought a high standard of passenger comfort on main line expresses.

However, Ireland was best known in railway enthusiast circles for the uniqueness of its narrow gauge railways. There was the efficient County Donegal Railway with its cherry red engines and red-and-cream railcars. The Cavan and Leitrim Railway had become a collecting point for usable stock from at least three other 3ft gauge lines. Even the West Clare had its charm, although it had been fully dieselised and was running in a somewhat desolate part of Ireland. These lines still survived in 1957 and so have their places in this book.

After 1956 a concerted drive took place in the north and central parts of Ireland to eliminate the most unremunerative routes, and thus several of the scenes illustrated in this album belong firmly in the past. The end of the Great Northern Railway, which resulted from either country taking over those tracks within its boundaries, has caused very great changes in recent years to the trains and services running on that section. The oddest feature of this change of ownership was the arbitrary, equal division of all rolling stock classes between the two countries and which in later years caused subsequent purchases by Ulster Transport of ex GN locomotives that had originally been allocated to CIE stock! Some of the photographs in this album have been included to illustrate the great contrast between the earlier trains and the latest diesel trains. These are now being painted in striking new liveries, helping to brighten the image of Irish railway transport.

It is the author's hope that readers who have known Ireland in the period covered by the album will recall their own pleasant memories of a very friendly country while browsing through its pages. Readers who have not known Ireland will probably be surprised that railways of such British character can possess features making them so distinctly Irish. This is helped by the rail gauges, as even 5ft 3in gauge looks broad to British eyes, permitting a more squat appearance to much of the rolling stock. On their steam locomotives the Irish almost universally preferred smokebox door wheels instead of the handles or other arrangements more popular in Great Britain—even English designs such as the Woolwich moguls and the Derby 2-6-4Ts sported these.

Even though steam traction has very nearly disappeared from Ireland, enthusiasts to whom all aspects of railways are interesting will still find a visit to Ireland worthwhile. The services offered by the railways, bearing in mind how thinly is the country populated, are very good and passenger travel is made pleasant by the clean and in many cases brightly painted stations, many of which use quite daring colours not seen this side of the Irish Sea. Cuisine at station restaurants and in refreshment cars is reasonably priced and of the high standard that food should be in a country where it is taken so seriously. Above all, there is the feeling that one is in a foreign country—the railways are different from our own and there are even differences from one side of the border to the other, notably in the sparcity of railways in the north compared with the results of the greater efforts made to maintain services on relatively rural lines in the south.

This album, however, emphasises the last memories of steam days on railways which can never be forgotten by people who knew them.

Long may their memory remain.

Irish railways offered some strange contrasts. Visually, CIE 1,200 hp diesel electric No A41, and SL&NCR 0-6-4T *Lough Melvin* are generations apart, yet they were actually delivered to Ireland within five years of one another, the diesel in 1956, and the 0-6-4T in 1951! This scene was photographed at Sligo in 1957, shortly before the Sligo, Leitrim line was closed.

A coal train from the mines at Dereenavoggy, near Arigna, to Belturbet passes Cornabrone Halt on the Arigna branch which ran for most of its length alongside the public road. The locomotive is No 4T, a Kerr Stuart 2-6-0T built for the Tralee and Dingle Railway in 1903. This scene on the Cavan and Leitrim was one of a series photographed by the author in 1957 with the help of the postmaster's bicycle hired from Ballinamore post office! The railway closed in April 1959.

Storming out of Belfast York Road station, one of Ulster Transport's successful Derby built 2-6-0s, No 91 *The Bush*, accelerates an express bound for Londonderry via the north coast route.

Great Northern Railway three-cylinder simple VS 4-4-0 No 208 *Lagan* struggles to start a heavy Belfast express out of Dublin Amiens Street station in 1956. These magnificent engines were the biggest 4-4-0s in Ireland and, introduced in 1948, were among the most modern GN locomotives.

Locomotives from three narrow gauge systems were still working on the Cavan and Leitrim section of CIE in 1957. This picture shows, from left to right, two C&LR 4-4-0Ts (background), Tralee and Dingle 2-6-0T No 3T, a Cork, Blackrock and Passage 2-4-2T, another Cavan and Leitrim 4-4-0T, and T&DR 2-6-0T No 4T resting at Ballinamore depot after a day's work.

The new black, gold and white livery applied to Coras Iompair Eireann locomotives and rolling stock in the 1960s is very striking and individualistic. It is shown here on General Motors 960 hp Bo-Bo diesel electric No B175 leaving Dublin Kingsbridge station in 1963 with an express for the south-west.

The Great Southern and Western Railway's most powerful passenger locomotives were the B1 4-6-0s designed by Bazin and introduced in 1924. Like the B2s, they ended their lives on freight duties, for which No 502 was being prepared at Cork Glanmire Road depot when this 1956 photograph was taken. The extra width resulting from the 5ft 3in rail gauge is noticeable at the front end.

After the First World War, the Midland and Great Western Railway sought to improve its services by purchasing from Woolwich Arsenal sets of parts of Maunsell's design for the English South Eastern and Chatham Railway N class. These were erected at Broadstone Works, though the majority entered service after the formation of the Great Southern Railways in 1925. They were identical to the SR N class, apart from gauge and detail variations, twenty being built to this design with 5ft 6in coupled wheels. A further six were also added in 1930 with 6ft wheels, and were thus similar to the Southern Railway's U class 2-6-0s. These locomotives were used all over the Great Southern (later CIE) system, particularly on the M&GWR and between Cork and Rosslare on the Fishguard boat trains.

Footplate view from Sligo, Leitrim and Northern Counties Railway 0-6-4T *Sir Henry* at Glenfarne, looking toward the border with Eire.

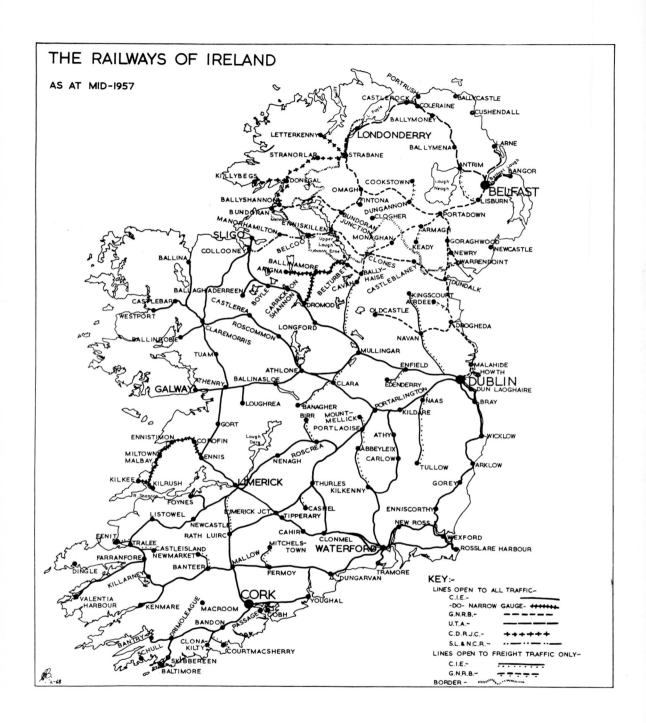

THE RAILWAYS OF IRELAND

AS AT MID-1957

KEY:-
LINES OPEN TO ALL TRAFFIC-
C.I.E.-
-DO- NARROW GAUGE- ++++++
G.N.R.B.-
U.T.A.-
C.D.R.J.C.- +++++++
S.L.&N.C.R.- — · — · —
LINES OPEN TO FREIGHT TRAFFIC ONLY-
C.I.E.-
G.N.R.B.-
BORDER -

Coras Iompair Eireann—Broad Gauge

IN 1956, all railway systems in Eire that did not cross the border with Northern Ireland were run by CIE. This national company also ran the majority of buses and road haulage vehicles in the Republic. A few years later, after the division of the Great Northern Railway and the closure of the County Donegal and SL&NCR lines, it had a virtual monopoly as far as railways in Eire were concerned.

CIE was formed in 1945 from the Great Southern Railways and the road transport constituents. The Great Southern in its turn had resulted from the 1925 amalgamation of the Great Southern and Western, the Midland and Great Western, the Dublin and South Eastern, the Cork, Bandon and South Coast and a number of narrow gauge railways. The Waterford, Limerick and Western had become part of the GS&WR after the turn of the century. These railway companies are specifically mentioned as photographs of some locomotives from each appear in this album.

From such a selection of railways, each with its own operating and engineering characteristics, it is not surprising that CIE before dieselisation was a fascinating railway for the enthusiast to tour.

Great Southern and Western Railway

The author's favourite CIE section, the GS&WR, covered the area between Dublin, Limerick, Tralee, Valentia Harbour, Cork, and Waterford. By 1956, the occasion of the author's first visit, trains on the Dublin to Cork and Limerick lines were already either diesel hauled (by Metro-Vick/Crossley 1,200 hp Co-Cos of class A) or were formed of diesel railcars. Steam traction was plentiful on the secondary routes and on main line freight trains.

By far the most ubiquitous steam locomotives, which were built from 1866 and survived in part until 1963, were the MacDonnell J15 0-6-0s of which 111 were built, by far the most numerous locomotives to run in Ireland. In their last days they were seen principally on the Dublin suburban services, on freight trains, beet specials, and on local passenger trains in the Cork area. That is where the author remembers them, both on the Cobh branch and on a stopping train from Cork to Killarney. They resembled the L&NWR Ramsbottom DXs, except for their larger boilers. The steady but slightly tinny exhaust beat of No 108 plodding up the 1 in 84 out of Cork on the main line was as pretty a sound as the engines were to look at.

Another almost unique feature of the GS&WR was that many of its Chief Mechanical Engineers later gained fame on British railways, but their Irish locomotives outlived many of their English ones! This applied to Aspinall, H. A. Ivatt, and Maunsell, and also to J. G. Robinson who had spent a period with the Waterford, Limerick and Western Railway.

Aspinall's lovely 4-4-0s of CIE's class D14 were still to be seen on Dublin suburban trains in 1957, and were the forerunners of many later, larger 4-4-0s built for the GS&WR to Coey's designs.

Ivatt had produced some quaint 2-4-2Ts which were still running to Cobh in 1956, and some solid 0-6-0Ts of good proportions that were at work in many parts of the system. One of these trundled a stock train through the street of Cork between the GS&WR and CB&SCR stations during the author's 1957 visit and thus stars in this album.

Only one of Robinson's locomotives, a 4-4-2T from the WL&WR, was seen by the author, and this was out of use among a group of derelict locomotives at Cork, Albert Quay.

The name of Maunsell was much better known lately in Ireland for his Woolwich moguls of which more anon, but one must not forget to mention *Sambo*. This was a Maunsell 0-4-2ST dating from 1913, a large but handsome machine for its type, which was for many years shunter at Inchicore Works, Dublin, and which still survived in 1963.

13

The lines in the western part of the GS&WR were very secondary in nature, all single track apart from the Cobh branch, and mostly worked in recent years by railcars, solid, comfortable diesels which rode well but sometimes smelled horribly of exhaust—indeed one could frequently wipe a thin film of soot off the ceiling in one of these! Valentia Harbour was the most westerly railway station in Europe until its closure when it passed this distinction to Camaret on the Réseau Breton.

Another winding, twisting route was that followed by the Cork boat trains from Rosslare, through Waterford to Mallow. These trains were last worked by Maunsell 2-6-0s until dieselisation. The boat train had for years a most excellent ex M&GWR clerestory 12-wheeled buffet car which served delicious breakfasts and which by 1963 CIE had honoured by painting it the new black, gold and white livery!

Previously to the black, gold and white, which is a most effective livery that looks good and does not show the dirt, CIE had a bad period with liveries. Dark green carriages were giving way to a pleasant light green by 1955 but this did not wear well. Diesel locomotives were being delivered in plain aluminium-silver, and unpainted coaches clad in stainless steel were being built in 1956-7 to match them, but the silver paint soon tarnished and began to look awful. The locomotives were therefore also painted light green from 1956, but looked drab.

The green did suit the three preserved steam locomotives, however, namely the little Bury 2-2-2 replica in Cork Glanmire Road station, the J15 0-6-0 No 184, and the biggest of them all, 4-6-0 No 800 *Maeve*. *Maeve* was one of the three giant 4-6-0s, nearly as big as GWR Kings, which the Great Southern introduced in 1939 to work the heaviest trains on the Dublin to Cork main line. They were utterly handsome machines, though much restricted in route availability. No 802 *Tailte* had been withdrawn by 1956, 800 *Maeve* was preserved that year, too, and 801 *Macha* disappeared about the same time. You can imagine the author's surprise therefore when, in 1957, he saw *Maeve* at Cork Glanmire Road depot in steam! Apparently CIE had struck a bad phase of non-availability of their A class diesels and No 800 had had to be purloined for a night Dublin to Cork freight. Also, the preserved 184 did some stirling work in the same period in the Dublin suburban area!

Midland and Great Western Railway

This large system covered central Ireland, fanning out westwards from Dublin to Galway, Ballina, and Sligo. It was less main line in character than the GS&WR, its principal routes being single track.

Of its older locomotives, the J18 and J19 0-6-0s were the nearest equivalent to the J15s and were to be seen everywhere on the system. They worked most freight and branch trains. Early passenger engines that survived until recently were the famous Atock G2 2-4-0s, beautiful little machines that were, according to reports, still working the Dublin-Galway main trains as late as 1957. One survived at Sligo until 1963. There were many 4-4-0s built later, but none outlived the last of the 2-4-0s and none was seen working on the author's visits in 1956 and 1957. Another unusual type was the J5 0-6-0, genuine mixed traffic engines with 5ft 8in wheels.

An interesting era in M&GWR motive power began in 1925, just as that railway became part of the GSR, when the first K1 2-6-0 emerged from the line's works at Broadstone, Dublin. Several kits of parts had been purchased by the M&GWR from Woolwich Arsenal which was making them for general sale to help relieve unemployment after the first world war. The Irish ones were 5ft 6in wheeled locomotives, virtually identical with the Southern Railway Maunsell N class but widened to the 5ft 3in rail gauge. Twenty were built, followed by a further six with 6ft coupled wheels similar to the SR U class. These worked the principal M&GW line passenger services, and also spread to the rest of the CIE system.

In recent years the Dublin terminus at Broadstone has been closed (it and the depot attached are now a road vehicle depot) and trains now run into the CIE side of Dublin (Amiens Street) station and cross the River Liffey on the overhead suburban line to terminate at Westland Row, the northern terminus of the Dublin and South Eastern section, thus affording physical connection with a wide area of CIE and ex GN railways.

Dublin and South Eastern Railway

This section of CIE consisted largely of the main line down the south east coast of Eire from Dublin (Westland Row) to Bray, Wicklow, Arklow, Wexford, and Rosslare Harbour. This also embraced the two suburban routes to Bray and Greystones from Dublin Harcourt Street (closed end 1958) and Westland Row stations.

A journey from Dublin to Rosslare made by the author in 1956 was of great interest even though speeds were low and stops were frequent. From Dublin through the outer suburbs several race-horse specials were observed including one hauled by an MGWR 2-4-0. The coastal section before Wicklow includes the hazardous stretch of line situated half way up the cliff face. Here there were several signs of route changes enforced by the receding cliff face including at one point two tunnels side by side, the one with a precipitous drop into the sea caused by erosion, the other having been bored a few yards inland to replace it. This route presumably ranks as one of Brunel's less successful. It also includes a stretch running along the beach near Wicklow, understood to be a section subject to frequent flooding. Further south near the Wicklow mountains the scenery is very pleasant and lush. There is a public street section with a severe speed restriction at Wexford before the line runs finally south east and on to the curved pier that forms Rosslare Harbour.

The author saw only four ex D&SER locomotives during his visits, all illustrated here, and none of these was actually on the DSE section. At Broadstone ex MGWR depot in 1956 were an 0-6-0 of class J8 and an interesting 2-6-0 with inside cylinders; a 4-4-2T was seen at Limerick in 1957, and a 2-4-2T, class F2, was among the derelict locomotives at the CB&SC depot at Cork. This latter locomotive had been exchanged for a Cork, Bandon 4-6-0T which the author had seen in use on the Dublin surburban lines.

Cork, Bandon and South Coast Railway

A single line started from Cork's Albert Quay station, climbed steeply into the hills, and ran a curvatious route, with little or no super elevation on curves, to Bantry, a beauty spot on Bantry Bay in the south west of County Cork. Two branches were thrown off southwards, one to Clonakilty and the other to Skibbereen and Baltimore. In 1957 the Cork-Bantry passenger trains were worked by a 3-car diesel railcar set and the branch trains were odd formations of 6-wheelers or ancient gas lit bogie coaches hauled by C class Metro-Vick 550 hp Bo-Bo diesel electrics.

Freight traffic was being taken over by C class diesels also, but a handful remained of the CB&SCR's excellent standard 4-6-0Ts of handsome appearance which had been produced by Beyer Peacock in 1906 to 1920. Most had superheated boilers but the author noted two that were non-superheated, No 470 in 1957 and No 463 in 1956.

A short branch line also turned off the Clonakilty branch and was originally known as the Timoleague and Courtmacsherry Railway. This included the only broad gauge roadside tramway in Ireland to carry passenger traffic, and although steam working had largely ceased by the time of the author's visits, three of the tiny locomotives used on it were still extant at Albert Quay depot. These were the ex T&CR 2-6-0T named *Argadeen* but never numbered, and ex GS&WR 0-6-0Ts Nos 100 and 299. No 100 was one of two diminutive survivors, the other being No 90. No 90 had been converted from its original state as an 0-6-4T rail motor and is now preserved at Fermoy station, whereas No 100 had been built as an 0-6-0T. No 299 was a small Hunslet 0-6-0ST.

The Modern CIE

CIE was completely dieselised by 1963 and after that year no steam locomotives remained in operating stock. The transformation of the railway during the last fifteen years has been outstanding. A somewhat decrepit, unpunctual, old fashioned railway has become one on which it is truly a pleasure to travel. Passenger facilities at stations, most of which have had facelifts in bold, bright colours, are good, there are restaurants available at most medium sized junctions, and the trains are smart, clean, comfortable, smooth riding, of adequate speed, and good punctuality.

In addition to the modernisation of stations, and in furtherance of Eire's policy of emphasising its historic position as a free state, many of CIE's main line stations have been renamed after Irish statesmen. This has had the strange effect of suppressing the well known station names of Kingsbridge,

Amiens Street and Westland Row in Dublin in favour of Heuston, Connolly, and Pearce stations respectively.

In CIE's dieselisation policies, the initial attempt to standardise on Metro-Vick/Crossley locomotives (60 A class and 33 C class were built) was not followed up. The early Sulzer locomotives, all grouped into class B in the 850-960 hp range, were not perpetuated either, and subsequent deliveries have been received from General Motors. Opinion at Inchicore Works in 1963 ran very highly in favour of the American machines as being low in maintenance, and reliable. The first batch of these 960 hp locomotives were obtained with single cabs, but all subsequent deliveries have appeared with a cab at each end, the engine room portion between the cabs being narrow in width, not contributing towards good looks but towards ease of access for maintenance. These are also classified in group B.

Most CIE shunting locomotives are of class E, built in Inchicore Works in two batches and incorporating Maybach engines and hydraulic transmissions.

The most interesting locomotive produced at Inchicore Works in recent years was Bulleid's 0-6-6-0T turf burning steam locomotive No CC1. This was substantially a development of his Leader class experiment on BR's Southern Region, but eliminating most of the Leader's weaknesses. It had two fabricated cylinders on each bogie driving a free crankshaft, with mechanically driven valve gear and piston valves, the chain drive being used only to couple the wheel sets to each other and to the crankshafts. The rectangular section boiler had a large central firebox and two barrels and smokeboxes to fore and aft. In the face of CIE's determined drive for dieselisation this interesting locomotive was not developed beyond the trial stage and in 1963 was standing among 30-odd other steam locomotives that were awaiting breaking up.

To the time of writing CIE has vigorously resisted the extensive closures of railways of the proportions that have occurred in the north and therefore offers a reasonable, countrywide service to all except the most remote areas. This has been achieved while attacking a deficit that has been held at a controlled level, and indications now are that CIE is all set to take its part in the fast developing economy of Eire.

Great Southern & Western Rly.

Left: A rare, if not unique, scene at Cork Glanmire Road motive power depot showing from left to right 550 hp Metrovick diesel No C215, Bredin class B1a 4-6-0 No 800 *Maeve* (a surprise visitor), a Coey D10 4-4-0, a Woolwich Mogul, a J15 0-6-0 and an Ivatt J11 0-6-0T, a group representing locomotive designs from 1866 to 1955.

Above: One of the ubiquitous class J15 0-6-0s, of which 111 were built between 1966 and 1903 to form Ireland's most numerous locomotive type, standing at Mallow on a Sunday excursion from Cork to Tralee in 1956.   As originally built this class were similar to the Ramsbottom DX class of the L&NWR in England, but No 108 in this photograph was one of the majority that were rebuilt with superheater boilers.

Right: CIE No 195, one of the non-superheated J15 0-6-0s, photographed at Cork in 1957.

17

Few passenger workings were left for the MacDonnell J15s by 1957, but in July No 140 was taking some turns on the Cobh branch. It is seen here leaving Cobh for Cork with a most attractive twelve wheeled clerestory vehicle at its head.

At the same time as No 140, a pair of Park Royal railcars was also on the Cobh run, pictured arriving from Cork. Each car had two AEC 125 hp diesel engines and five-speed gearboxes with a two-ratio final drive that could be set for high speed or suburban working. In order to be compatible with standard locomotive hauled stock the railcars were fitted with vacuum brakes and some had steam boilers for train heating. They were introduced in 1953.

An early Aspinall 4-4-0, class D17 No 18 stands derelict at Limerick. Many of these and his later D14s outlived his later engines built for the Lancashire and Yorkshire Railway.

The Ivatt Engines

The Cork City Railways were a small network of lines running through the City's streets connecting Glanmire Road station (Great Southern and Western Railway) and Albert Quay station (Cork, Bandon and South Coast Railway) with a number of quays in the docks area. In this photograph, ex GS&WR J11 0-6-0T No 217 hauls freight and empty passenger stock (6-wheelers) from Glanmire Road to Albert Quay.

Another view of 0-6-0T No 217 as it approaches Cork, Albert Quay station via the Cork City Railways. With its six-wheeled coaches nicely humped over the bridge, it forms a pleasant picture of the Irish 5ft 3in gauge.

Between 1887 and 1901 H. A. Ivatt introduced onto the GS&WR a class of 0-6-0Ts that became CIE class J11 and which outlived all his later English locomotives. No 207, photographed at Cork in 1956, was one of the class which did not receive the later single piece smokebox door but retained double doors.

In September 1955 the Ivatt class F6 2-4-2Ts of the GS&WR were still to be seen in the Cork area. Here, No 34 leaves Cork Glanmire Road with the 5.20pm to Cobh formed of six-wheeled stock.

[*R.Stieber*

22

Top: Ivatt's very attractive F6 2-4-2Ts were built between 1892 and 1894 and in later years worked in the Cork suburban area to Cobh, Youghal, and Macroom.   No 33 was one of a number still working on the CB&SC section of CIE in 1956.

Bottom: Only one year later diesel locomotives were on the scene on Cork suburban traffic.   The author made a journey from Cork to Youghal in July 1957 behind an A class Co-Co hauling fourteen six-wheeled coaches!   His return train is illustrated at Youghal formed of C class Bo-Bo No C217 well overloaded with ten coaches, eight of which were six-wheelers.   Six-wheeled stock for passenger traffic had disappeared from CIE by the author's 1963 visit.

Coey

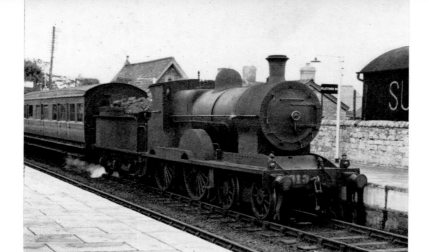

Ready to leave Thurles, on the Dublin-Cork main line, with a train for Clonmel on the Waterford-Limerick line, class D10 4-4-0 No 313 is ample power for its two gas lit coaches. The D10s were one of many successful passenger engines designed by R. Coey for the GS&WR in the first decade of this century.

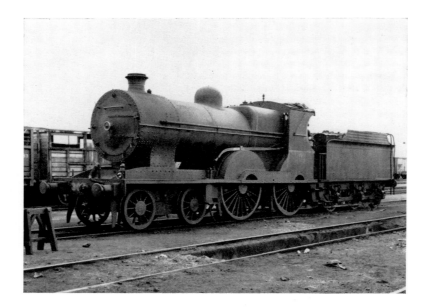

Coey 4-4-0 No 307 of class D12 at Thurles in 1956.

The class D4 4-4-0s were a mixed traffic design with 5ft 8½in coupled wheels. No 344 was one of a number which were unusual in having outside framed bogies.

Engines

The simple lines of Coey's goods 0-6-0s are evident in this view of J4 No 263 at Mallow.

A lighter 0-6-0 was the class J9, like No 251 seen here at Limerick in 1956.

Originally designed as 0-6-0s, found too heavy at the front and rebuilt as 2-6-0s, the K4s were Coey's most powerful freight locomotives. No 361 was photographed at Mallow in 1956.

The only J. G. Robinson engine seen during any of the author's visits was ex Waterford, Limerick and Western Railway 4-4-2T No 269, seen at Cork Albert Quay depot in 1957.

The last surviving R. E. L. Maunsell locomotive in Ireland was ex GS&WR 0-4-2T *Sambo*, Inchicore Works shunting engine, photographed there in 1963 awaiting breaking up.

MacDonnell J15s predominate in this view of Tralee motive power depot. On the extreme left is a Maunsell class K1 2-6-0 which had arrived earlier with a special from Dublin. Steam disappeared from this area only a few years after this 1957 photograph.

An evening scene at Tralee with Metro-vick Co-Co No A19 about to leave on the day's last train to Dublin. The train stabled in the through platform (right) includes one of the then new stainless steel clad four-wheeled boiler vans provided for train heating, the diesel locomotives not being so equipped.

Opposite top: Of impressive appearance, though simple in outline, were the class B1 4-6-0s of the GS&WR. No 502 was photographed at Cork Glanmire Road depot in 1956.

Above: The Bury 2-2-2 replica of No 36 which stands on view at Cork Glanmire Road station.

Opposite bottom: The biggest steam locomotives in Ireland were the three Bredin class B1a three-cylinder 4-6-0s built in 1939 to 1940 for the Dublin to Cork mail trains. Introduced just as war broke out in Europe, these locomotives, second only to the GWR Kings for size, hardly had any opportunity to show their paces. For a short while in the early 1950s they worked the Enterprise expresses between Dublin and Cork for the brief time that those trains provided a through service from Belfast to Cork. They ended their lives on freight services. No 800 was restored with double chimney in 1955 and surprisingly was put into service on a Dublin to Cork freight duty in 1957, when this photograph was taken at Cork. It has since been preserved at the transport museum at Belfast.

Midland and Great Western Railway

Immediately before dieselisation of the M&GW section main line trains the Maunsell Woolwich 2-6-0s of classes K1 and K1a were the line's top express engines. In this view No 373 approaches Athlone from Dublin with a train for Galway, including in its formation two travelling post office vehicles with pick-up nets. The fourth vehicle on the train is an ex Pullman car, one or two of which were still extant in 1956.   [R. Stieber

Above: The Midland and Great Western had its own equivalents to the J15s of the GS&WR. These were Atock's class J18 and J19 0-6-0s built between 1876 and 1895. They were basically similar engines and with round-topped and Belpaire boiler freely interchanged between them they were distinguishable only by detail differences. No 594 in this photograph at Sligo belonged to class J18.

Below: Class J19 0-6-0 No 583 was among a group of last survivors awaiting cutting up at Mullingar in 1963.

Between 1893 and 1898 a series of 2-4-0 passenger locomotives (later known as class G2) was introduced on the Midland and Great Western Railway by M. Atock. These were the last 2-4-0s to remain in regular passenger work in the British Isles as they survived until the early 1960s. The last was still at Sligo in summer 1963! Among their first and last duties were the nightly Dublin to Galway mail trains. No 665 in this photograph was pausing at Bray on a Dublin and South Eastern section racehorse special, in August 1956.

The only reason for the existence of Atock class D16 4-4-0 No 532 as late as summer 1957 was that it had been in use as a stationary boiler at Broadstone motive power depot, Dublin. This class, introduced in 1900, failed to survive the success of the older G2 2-4-0s which were, in fact, more powerful locomotives.

The Morton J5 0-6-0s may well have been the largest wheeled 0-6-0s in Great Britain and Eire. Their 5ft 8in coupled wheels gave them a good turn of speed and they were frequently seen on passenger trains, even at times on Dublin to Dun Laoghaire boat trains!

The locomotive depot at Mullingar in 1955, with J5 0-6-0 No 639 on the left, and J18 No 594. [R. Stieber

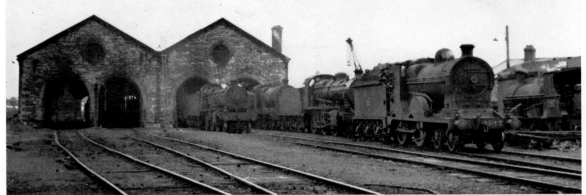

The Dublin terminus of the Midland and Great Western Railway was at Broadstone.   By 1956 the station area had become a road bus depot.   The motive power depot by the station was still in use in the late fifties.   This 1957 photograph includes one of the few remaining D6 4-4-0s that shared some M&GW section duties with the Woolwich 2-6-0s, two of which are evident in this view.   By 1963 however the depot and all tracks in the vicinity had disappeared and the area was in use as a CIE road transport depot.   [R. Stieber

One of CIEs enterprising types of excursion involved special trains of stock fitted with public address that could be used to give commentaries on places of interest on a journey to one of many of the attractive parts of western Ireland.   The photograph shows a class K1 2-6-0 leaving Athlone with a Radio Train for Galway.   [R. Stieber

The standard shunting locomotive of the MGWR was Atock's 0-6-0T of CIE class J26, built 1891 to 1893. One of the last to survive was No 562, here seen at Inchicore Works, Dublin, awaiting breaking up in 1963.

After main line services between Dublin and Cork had been dieselised by CIE in 1956 later deliveries of the Metrovick 1,200 hp Co-Cos began work on the Midland and Great Western section. This 1956 shot shows No A51 arriving at Dromod with a train from Dublin Westland Row to Sligo.

Dublin and South Eastern Railway

Above: Many Dublin and South Eastern section services started from Westland Row station in the south of Dublin's busy city centre. In this view an ex M&GWR 0-6-0T is shunting while Metrovick/Crossley diesel No A39 pauses after arrival from the north west with an M&GW section train.

Left: Two Dublin and South Eastern Railway goods locomotives at Broadstone depot in 1956. In the centre is Cronin J8 0-6-0 No 444 and on the left background is one of the two Wild class K2 inside cylinder 2-6-0s that were largely employed on freight workings on the DSE and MGW sections. The 0-6-0s were introduced in 1904 and the 2-6-0s in 1922.

In the 1950s Dublin and South Eastern 2-4-2T No 432, one of a class built 1886 to 1898, was sent to work on the Cork, Bandon and South Coast section.   By 1956 it was out of use, stored in the locomotive yard at Cork Albert Quay.

This Cronin class C2 4-4-2T, CIE No 457, was photographed in inactive condition, well away from its home, at Limerick in 1957.

Even as late as 1957 the Aspinall 4-4-0s of the GS&WR were still to be seen on suburban passenger trains in the Dublin area. Class D14 4-4-0 No 89 is pictured at Westland Row on a train from Amiens Street to Bray.

Dublin

Another D14, No 62, passing through Westland Row in 1956 with a train of empty suburban stock. This class, built between 1885 and 1895, outlived all of Aspinall's later locomotives built for the Lancashire and Yorkshire Railway.

The J15 0-6-0s also had their turns at suburban work.   No 122 is seen on the overhead railway section between Amiens Street, Tara Street and Westland Row.

Suburban

The only suburban tank engines in regular use in recent years in the Dublin area were the Harty class I3 0-6-2Ts introduced by the Great Southern Railways in 1933.   No 671 is seen arriving with a heavy train at Westland Row.

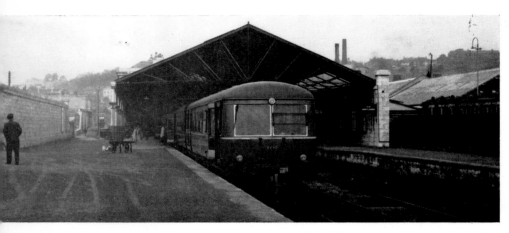

Above: A view of the small terminus at Cork Albert Quay from which ran the passenger services of the Cork, Bandon and South Coast section of CIE.

Cork, Bandon and South Coast Railway

Opposite page: On the Cork, Bandon and South Coast Railway section, a branch train from Baltimore to Drimoleague approaches Skibbereen behind Metrovick/Crossley 550 hp Bo-Bo diesel electric locomotive No C202.

Below: During the last few years of services on the CB&SCR passenger trains between Cork and Bantry were worked by a three car diesel mechanical unit. Branch passenger and freight trains were dealt with largely by 550 hp C class diesel electrics. This photograph shows, right, the daily train from Cork to Bantry connecting with, left, a branch train to Skibbereen and Baltimore, at Drimoleague in 1957.

Top: Until dieselisation the main line freight and passenger services on the CB&SCR were worked by a group of Beyer Peacock 4-6-0Ts built between 1906 and 1920. No 470 is at Albert Quay depot, Cork.

Centre: All but two of the B4 4-6-0Ts from the Cork, Bandon and South Coast Railway were rebuilt with superheater boilers. No 464, one of the superheated ones, was in use at Inchicore Works in 1963 as a stationary boiler.

Bottom: A fascinating assortment at Albert Quay depot, Cork. Reading from left to right:—Back row: A Cork, Bandon and South Coast Railway 4-6-0T; Hunslet 0-6-0ST No 299 which the Great Southern and Western Railway used on the lightly laid Timoleague and Courtmacsherry Railway; and 2-6-0T *Argadeen* of the aforesaid T&CR. Middle row: A Midland and Great Western Railway 0-6-0T of class J26; and a Waterford, Limerick and Western Railway 4-4-2T designed by J. G. Robinson before he moved to the Great Central Railway in England. Front row: A CB&SCR 4-6-0T; and an Ivatt F6 2-4-2T from the GS&WR.

A 5ft 3in gauge light railway branched off the Clonakilty branch at Ballinascarty and had the name: Timoleague and Courtmacsherry Railway. The last surviving loco-motive of the T&CR was 2-6-0T *Argadeen,* unnumbered, seen here at Cork Albert Quay locomotive depot in 1955. It was still in the identical spot when seen by the author two years later. *[R. Stieber*

Timoleague and Courtmacsherry Railway

Two diminutive 0-6-0Ts also worked on the T&C section although originally belonging to the GS&WR. No 90 was one of three originally built as 0-6-4T rail motors used on the Castleisland branch and for the Inchicore Works to Kingsbridge shuttle service. Later rebuilt as an 0-6-0T No 90 was finally preserved and sited at Fermoy station. The Fermoy and Mitchelstown line had in fact been worked by two similar locomotives built as 0-6-0Ts without the carriage portion. Of these, No 100 was still in use on the CB&SC section as station pilot at Albert Quay as late as 1957. The photographs show, above, No 90 at Fermoy in 1963 after restoration in GS&WR livery, and, below, No 100 at Cork in 1955.

[Photo of No 100 by R. Stieber

Another ex GS&WR engine to be employed for a time on the Timoleague and Courtmacsherry branch was Hunslet 0-6-0ST No 299 which also ended its days with a long sojourn at the back of the locomotive yard at Cork.

By 1955 the use of diesel railcars had made an impact on the standard of CIE passenger services, even though some of the trailer coaches they were matched with were somewhat ancient by comparison. This scene inside Dublin's Westland Row station in 1957 shows the evening train to Sligo preparing for departure.

The Modern CIE

With tablet catchers at the ready for single line working, class A diesel electric No A37 pauses at Athenry with a Dublin to Galway main line freight.

Above: In the early 1950s two Sulzer engined 860 hp Bo-Bo diesel electric locomotives were constructed at Inchicore, Nos 1100 and 1101. They were employed mainly on freight services on the Dublin to Cork main line. The photograph shows the second of them, renumbered B114, at Inchicore in 1963 after having been repainted in black, gold and white. On the left of the photograph can just be seen the cab of an A class locomotive in the old silver livery, much worn, and the C class Bo-Bo on the right of the picture is in the interim shade of green.

Opposite page: Not only steam locomotives produce smoke effects! One of the Metropolitan Vickers Co-Co locomotives with Crossley 1,200 hp two-stroke diesel engines, No A25, pulls out of Cork's Glanmire Road station with a Sunday excursion in 1956. In 1968 two of these locomotives are being re-engined with 1,325 hp General Motors engines for trial to determine the suitability of this power unit for the ultimate re-engining of the whole class.

Below: In 1956 delivery began of a batch of twelve 960 hp Sulzer A1A-A1As from the Birmingham Railway Carriage and Wagon Co. to CIE. Being in the power range between 850 and 1,000 hp these diesel electrics were classed in group B. No B102 was photographed on the Sunday train from Cork to Dublin at Mallow, shortly after entering service.

With a view to complete dieselisation of lightly laid secondary lines and branches, CIE ordered 33 of these 550 hp diesel electrics from Metropolitan-Vickers, delivery of which began in earnest in 1957. Being of low power they were not ideally suited to general mixed traffic work, and could not have been economical on such workings as that in the photograph—a branch train from Baltimore at Drimoleague on the Cork, Bandon section of CIE. In 1967 two of this class were re-engined with Maybach 980 hp diesel engines, and CIE are equipping two further with 1,000 hp General Motors engines. Six-wheeled coaches as seen in this view had disappeared from the CIE scene by 1963.

The most successful CIE main line diesel locomotives have been the two groups of 960 hp diesel electrics built in America by General Motors. An example of the first delivery, 5ft 3in gauge version of a standard American road switcher, is No B132 here seen at Dublin Kingsbridge after being released from a Limerick to Dublin service.

The last and strangest steam locomotive built at Inchicore Works was O. V. Bulleid's 0-6-6-0T turf burner No CC1. It is here seen at Inchicore, Dublin, in 1963 in unusual company: ex Cork, Bandon and South Coast 4-6-0T No 463 waiting breaking up, and an ex Great Northern Railway locomotive tender from a condemned class U 4-4-0.

Dislike in Ireland of the single ended locomotive for main line service led to later deliveries of the General Motors Bo-Bos being produced with full width cabs at each end. Here, No B174 arrives at Portarlington with the 10.00 from Kingsbridge to Limerick, in 1963. It is in the new black, gold and white colours of CIE, though most of its train is still in the earlier light green.

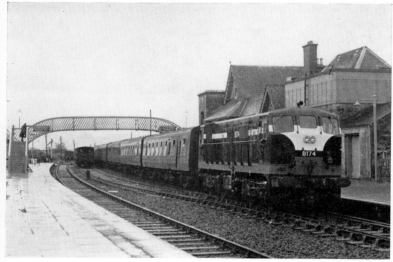

In 1956 CIE built at Inchicore some 400 hp diesel hydraulic shunting locomotives of their own design. They were equipped with Maybach engines and hydraulic transmission and were identified as group E.

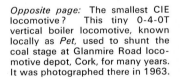

Later locomotives of the E class were built in the early 1960s and were of neater appearance but basically the same machine. No E430 was photographed in 1963 shunting at the ex Great Northern station at Amiens Street, Dublin.

Opposite page: The smallest CIE locomotive? This tiny 0-4-0T vertical boiler locomotive, known locally as *Pet*, used to shunt the coal stage at Glanmire Road locomotive depot, Cork, for many years. It was photographed there in 1963.

In an attempt to determine whether lightly laid freight-only branch lines could be economically worked by one-man-operated diesel locomotives, CIE purchased in 1956 three 160 hp Deutz 0-4-0 diesel hydraulics. With these the Newmarket and Castleisland branches were reopened and a minimum service run for a few years before final closure took place. Further similar locomotives were added to the fleet in later years and No G616 was one of these.

Coras Iompair Eireann—Narrow Gauge

IRELAND WAS well known in the past as being a happy hunting ground for enthusiasts of the narrow gauge. The relative poverty of its rural areas could support little else, but these little railways have taken a heavy toll and disappeared completely. The Cork and Muskerry Light Railway, the Cork, Blackrock and Passage, and the Schull and Skibbereen showed no trace and the Tralee and Dingle had been pulled up before the author reached Ireland. Two lines survived until 1959, the Cavan and Leitrim and the West Clare. No two 3ft gauge railways under one management could surely have been so different in character.

Cavan and Leitrim Railway

On the map the Cavan and Leitrim looked like a letter T with Dromod, and the Dublin-Sligo line, at its base, Ballinamore at the junction in the centre, Belturbet (junction with the Great Northern) on the right, and Arigna on the left of the T.

It was most usually reached via Dromod where, at the small platform behind and out of sight of the main station, one would usually find a strange looking train headed by an ungainly, large wheeled 2-4-2T inherited from the Cork, Blackrock and Passage Railway. A modern, all steel passenger coach made from sections of two bus bodies on a Tralee and Dingle bogie underframe, and a series of assorted goods vans and a brake van formed the train. The train would pull out of Dromod and head north at a steady pace not exceeding 25 miles per hour. Up the many steep hills the engine would clank loudly, occasionally nearly slipping to a standstill near the top, and would run freely down the other side, approaching each level crossing with caution and with prolonged shrieks on its piercing whistle to ensure someone from the crossing keeper's cottage came out to open the gates. Swinging down into Ballinamore the 'main line' ran alongside the Arigna branch which came in from the left, into the station of the small town that was the hub of the Cavan and Leitrim.

Here were the main locomotive depot and the workshops of the system, staffed by loyal men whose combined skill and improvisation kept the railway staggering through its last few years until the inevitable closure.

Here also started the daily Arigna mixed train. This would normally have one of the graceful Cavan and Leitrim 4-4-0Ts at its head, or a chunky ex Tralee and Dingle 2-6-0T. The 2-4-2Ts and the T&DR No 5 2-6-2T normally stayed on the 'main line'. The Arigna train looked weird to British eyes. With cowcatcher to fore and a really superb, if disintegrating, clerestory, platform ended bogie coach, the train's appearance was reminiscent in some ways of the American west. This train would leave Ballinamore heading west, clatter across the level crossing at the bottom of the town's main street, and, after a mile or two, join the public road alongside which it would run most of the way to Arigna. This road is far from level or straight but the Arigna branch followed all but its most violent curves and gradients! In July 1957 activity on the Arigna branch was intense, for the Dereenavoggy coal quarries at the Arigna end were working for their holiday bonus and up to four coal trains a day were being run. These ran through principally to Belturbet where the coal was transhipped by hand into broad gauge wagons at the GNR station. The Belturbet line was similar in character to that from Dromod.

To the author, the Cavan and Leitrim was the most Irish of all Irish railways. It was an earnestly run unit that had fate set against it. When a power station was built close by the Dereenavoggy mines the coal no longer needed to search for distant markets and the raison d'être of the line just vanished, closure being effected in April 1959. Its memory however never will vanish among those who have known it, particularly in America at Pleasure Island, Wakefield, Massachusetts where 4-4-0T No 3L, 2-6-2T No 5T and a bogie coach have been preserved by the Lady Edith Society!

West Clare Railway

By the time the author reached it, in 1957, the West Clare had been woken up. Running in a desolate part of western Eire to the harsh Atlantic coast, it made a last ditch stand for survival under the auspieces of CIE.

Three diesel railcar hauled trains a day ran from Ennis to Kilkee or Kilrush connecting at Ennis with the broad gauge route from Limerick to Galway and Sligo whose train service was at best two passenger workings a day in each direction.   The three foot gauge railcars had been supplied by Walker Bros. of Wigan to the same design as the last County Donegal cars and they were given passenger trailers of the bus body type.   They ran smartly between stops and reached speeds of up to 35 mph.   The peculiar jangling of their coupling rods, and their klaxon horns gave these strange little trains an exciting atmosphere of their own.

Even freight trains had been provided with diesel locomotives, the only ones on the Irish narrow gauge with one exception.   These West Clare machines were centre cab locomotives of B-B arrangement running on power bogies identical with railcar driving bogies, an excellent example of standardisation.

A few miles from its west end the West Clare line split in two at a spot called Moyasta Junction. The left hand leg continued the few miles to the small port of Kilrush on the Shannon estuary, and the right hand line ended at the tiny, wind-swept holiday resort of Kilkee.   Through trains to Kilrush were met by connections at Moyasta for Kilkee and vice versa, full use being made of the triangular layout at the junction to turn the railcars which were unidirectional.

Two of the steam locomotives used on the West Clare Railway were still at Inchicore in 1957 after taking part in a film, but had disappeared a year later.   After final closure of the line talk was rife for a time that the Isle of Man Railway was considering aquisition of a number of the three diesel locomotives, but no purchase was made and these were still intact, together with the driving ends of two of the railcars, at Inchicore in 1963.   Many who regret the passing of the narrow gauge will be glad that the West Clare at least went down kicking!

Platform scene at Ballinamore as ex Tralee and Dingle Railway 2-6-2T No 5T prepares to leave with a train for Dromod, on the Dublin-Sligo main line of the M&GWR. No 5T was built at Hunslet's in 1892, and was photographed in 1956, on the Cavan and Leitrim section of CIE. The locomotive has since been shipped to the United States of America for preservation.

After arrival from Dromod, 2-4-2T No 10L prepares to leave Ballinamore with the 2 pm mixed train to Belturbet. The locomotive is one of four transferred from the Cork, Blackrock and Passage Railway in 1934 and used on the Cavan and Leitrim section's " main line " between Dromod, Ballinamore and Belturbet. The coach consists of an ex Tralee and Dingle bogie vehicle underframe with a modern body provided by CIE.

Cavan and

Outside the depot and workshops at Ballinamore, two narrow gauge tank locomotives pause after the day's work. Left is ex Tralee and Dingle Railway 2-6-0T No 3T and on the right is Cavan and Leitrim 4-4-0T No 4L, built by Stephenson's in 1887. The engines built for the C&LR had unusually large fireboxes, reportedly so that they could burn the relatively poor indigenous Arigna coal, though in later years imported coal was in fact used.

[R. Stieber

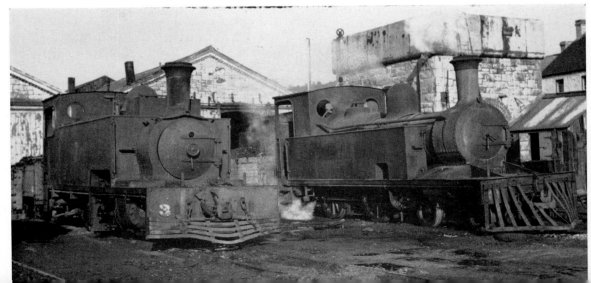

The interior of the workshops at Ballinamore with, left, C&L 4-4-0T No 4L and, right, ex T&DR 2-6-2T No 5T.

Leitrim Railway

In the bay platform at Ballinamore, 2-6-0T No 3T waits to depart with the daily mixed train to Arigna.   The old clerestory coaches with end platforms appear very foreign, but were in use on the Arigna branch until closure.

Above: An empty coal train bound for Arigna curves sharply down and away from the " main line " to Dromod and approaches the level crossing at the bottom of Ballinamore's main street. The locomotive is Cavan and Leitrim 4-4-0T No 3L, originally named *Lady Edith* and now preserved in America. This photograph was taken in the summer of 1957.

Opposite page top: The daily Arigna branch mixed train on the Cavan and Leitrim section pauses at Drumshambo to take water and to effect remedial measures on a warm bogie axlebox on the locomotive, Cavan and Leitrim Railway 4-4-0T No 2L built by Stephensons in 1887. Photographed in 1957.

Opposite page bottom: The station yard at Arigna with No 2L preparing to move the return mixed train into the platform.

The scene on the Arigna road as ex Tralee and Dingle 2-6-0T No 4T makes its leisurely way towards Ballinamore with a coal train.

The north eastern terminus of the Cavan and Leitrim section of CIE was at Belturbet where an end-on connection was made with a short branch from the Great Northern Railway's route from Clones to Cavan. On the left of this scene 2-4-2T No 10L pulls away with a short mixed train for Ballinamore. The platform on the right is occupied by the 5ft 3in gauge coach and van which formed the Belturbet-Ballyhaise shuttle service of the GNR.

The view ahead from the cab of ex CB&PR 2-4-2T No 10L at
Dromod, Cavan and Leitrim section.

The scene at Ennis station as the morning broad gauge CIE train from Limerick to Galway arrives behind a class A Co-Co and connects with a West Clare section railcar for Kilrush standing in the bay platform.

West Clare Railway

The diesel railcars which CIE introduced on the 3ft gauge West Clare Railway were almost identical to the CDR cars Nos 19 and 20.   No 3388 is pictured at Ennistimon en route from Ennis to Kilrush in 1957.

Every railcar arriving at Moyasta Junction was met with a connection so that Kilrush and Kilkee were equally well served by trains from Ennis. On the right of this view railcar No 3388 has arrived from Ennis and is bound for Kilrush, and on the left is No 3389 ready to depart for Kilkee.

A morning train from Ennis arrives at the tiny seaside resort of Kilkee on the Atlantic coast.

The railcars used on the West Clare section were built by Walker Bros. of Wigan and were based on the successful vehicles used on the County Donegal Railways. CIE refurbished some bogie coaches for use as trailers. The train in this photograph is preparing to leave the port of Kilrush for Ennis.

When the West Clare became fully dieselised, freight services were taken over by three B-B diesel mechanical locomotives also built by Walker Bros. of Wigan. Each locomotive had two powered bogies identical to the power bogie of a railcar. No F503 was photographed at Miltown Malbay in 1957.

The last West Clare section steam locomotives were still at Ennis in 1955. No 2C, a Hopkins 2-6-2T was photographed there inside the locomotive depot.　　[R. Stieber

Two of the better known types of West Clare Railway steam locomotives were seen at Inchicore in 1957 after being involved in film making. On the left is one of the Hopkins 0-6-2Ts with unusually large trailing wheels, and on the right is a Carter 4-6-0T.　　[R. Stieber

The Great Northern Railway

IRELAND'S TWO greatest cities, Dublin and Belfast, were linked by the Great Northern Railway, which also served the border country westwards to Bundoran and north to Londonderry.

The Great Northern Railway's management had never allowed their railway to become in any way decrepit. Trains were smart, staff morale was high, station working efficient and timekeeping as good as the vagaries of customs examinations would permit. Its express locomotives were all fine steam locomotives, painted a cheerful shade of blue with black and white lining and deep red valances and buffer beams; these looked well against the well-maintained "golden teak" rolling stock.

On the Dublin-Belfast main line heavy express trains loading up to twelve bogie coaches were hauled at surprising speeds by majestic 4-4-0s of three principal types. The largest and latest were the five VS 3-cylinder simple 4-4-0s of the 1948 built River class, handsome engines with neat smoke deflectors. These were derived from the pre-war Glover compound 4-4-0s of class V, equally good machines named after birds. A smaller group of inside cylinder 4-4-0s, classes S and S2, frequently worked main line expresses also.

The crack trains were the Enterprise non-stops, two of which ran daily in each direction between Dublin and Belfast when the author first visited the Great Northern. The Belfast based train was hauled by a VS 4-4-0 and composed of eight coaches of the latest, most comfortable stock. The Dublin based set was in 1956 a 4-car railcar unit, composed of two of the Great Northern's early AEC railcars with two standard carriages in between, all painted in an attractive blue and cream. New, more powerful railcars were brought into use on this train the following year. On normal trains on the main line customs examinations were carried out at lengthy stops at Dundalk and Goraghwood stations. The Enterprise trains however were non-stops, and special arrangements were made for customs examinations at Dublin and Belfast.

The main line started in the GNR terminus section of Dublin's Amiens Street station and ran northwards near the east coast, crossing a wide bay on a lengthy causeway at Malahide. At Drogheda a large bridge, designed for single track, took the main line across the River Boyne; the double tracks were gauntletted across the bridge to avoid the need for points at each end. The main workshops of the GNRB were situated at Dundalk, north of which the main line began climbing through rugged countryside to cross the border hills before running down to Goraghwood and Portadown, and continuing thence through the suburbs into Belfast (Great Victoria Street station).

The GNR also ran one of the two competing routes from Belfast to Londonderry which left the main line at Portadown and ran westwards through some hilly country via Dungannon, Omagh and Strabane where connection was made with the County Donegal Railways. South from Omagh ran another route to Enniskillen (junction for the SL&NCR), Clones in Eire, and Dundalk, and a line linked Portadown with Clones via Armagh. These secondary routes were worked variously by railcars and a variety of excellent 4-4-0s mostly of the GT Clifford family. Goods engines were principally 0-6-0 versions of the 4-4-0s.

Two branch lines are worthy of particular note. One struck westwards from Ballyhaise on the Clones-Cavan line and ran about ten miles to its terminus at Belturbet where its one-coach passenger train shared a half island platform with the narrow gauge Cavan and Leitrim line. The GN's Belturbet branch was worked by a charming 2-4-2T which now rests at Belfast's transport museum.

The other branch worthy of note was that from Fintona Junction, on the Omagh-Enniskillen line, to Fintona, half a mile away. This was the province of the famous Fintona horse tram. This aged vehicle carried third class passengers in the open on top (fare 1d), first class in whichever half downstairs was to the rear, and second class downstairs in front—immediately behind the horse! This line closed in 1957, the tram retired to Belfast Transport Museum, and the horse—Dick—retired to a leisurely life in a nearby field!

North of Dublin there is a small peninsular formed mainly by the Hill of Howth, a popular scenic and holiday spot. The Great Northern Railway ran a tramway over this hill until recently, from Sutton over the hill to Howth, both ends connecting with stations on the Howth branch. One of the electric open top 5ft 3in gauge trams is now preserved in England at the tram museum at Crich in Derbyshire.

The Modern Great Northern

In 1958 the Great Northern Railway Board was dissolved by both governments and divided between them. The railway and fixed assets north of the border went to the Ulster Transport Authority and those south of the border to Coras Iompair Eireann. Locomotives and rolling stock were equally divided, class by class. On CIE the locomotives retained their GNR numbers, plus the suffix N. The UTA renumbered into its own fleet those locomotives which it intended to work for some time, the remainder retaining their GNR numbers with an X suffix. The initials UT or CIE were stencilled on buffer beams as appropriate. Railcars were renumbered into their new owners' respective lists.

From the start, through running of steam locomotives, except on special trains, ceased on the Belfast-Dublin line, all regular trains changing engines at Dundalk on the CIE side of the border. Those trains that were composed of diesel railcars however did work through. Variety of carriage stock livery was the order of the day, even as late as 1963, with the following styles all capable of being present at one and the same time: GNR teak, GNR blue and cream, UTA dark green, CIE light green, and CIE black, gold and white! GNR locomotives on the Ulster side began emerging from York Road Works in UTA black, but CIE, still pushing ahead with dieselisation, preferred to run down its stock of GN engines until by 1963 all had been displaced by diesels. CIE virtually began to run the GN lines as an integral part of their whole system, and diesel locomotives and rolling stock were freely circulated everywhere.

North of the border UTA tended to treat the GN lines as a separate railway, apart from introducing to it a number of their excellent Derby 2-6-0s and 2-6-4Ts, and ex NCC section railcars were not seen south of Belfast.

With the division of the GNR several other routes were split, apart from the main line, and the UTA very quickly closed these as uneconomic, virtually forcing CIE to act likewise with the truncated remains south of the border. Also, having two routes to Londonderry, the UTA rationalised by closing the ex GN route from Portadown in 1964 thus leaving the main line and the Lisburn-Antrim freight branch as the sole remains of the GNR north of the border.

In 1966 arrangements were begun for the railway interests of the UTA to be vested in a limited company to be known as Northern Ireland Railways Co. Ltd. The first outward evidence of the change was the introduction of a new, brighter livery for passenger trains, namely crimson and off white, which is considerably more attractive than the old dark green.

One effect of the division of interests appears to be that, whereas the old GNR used vigorously to promote passenger travel between the two countries and ran many long trains on the cross border routes, neither CIE nor NIR gives very great prominence to the Dublin-Belfast main line in their literature (indeed the NIR 1967/68 winter timetable shows it as non-existent south of Portadown). An apparent result is that at the author's last visit in 1967 only four through trains ran between the two capitals each weekday and these were only four or six car formations. This service was operated by two train sets, CIE providing a diesel locomotive hauled train (the locomotive worked right through to Belfast) and NIR an ex GNR four car railcar set. Each train did two return trips dubbed "Enterprise Expresses" even though half of them incorporated stops at Dundalk and Portadown. This was undoubtedly an economic way of running the service and was quite adequate to meet the meagre traffic offering, with fast schedules of two hours, ten or fifteen minutes each way. But the splendid character of the old Great Northern Railway had gone. Its independent spirit and its fine locomotives now remain a memory.

Above: One of the fine Glover compound three cylinder 4-4-0s of class V, No 86 *Peregrine*, standing at Adelaide locomotive depot, Belfast. The GNRB crest appeared both on the tender and on the splasher beneath the nameplate.

Below: When more top line passenger locomotives were needed after the last war five VS simple 4-4-0s were introduced by Beyer Peacock in 1948. No 207 *Boyne* was photographed at Adelaide in 1957, and was eventually the last survivor of the class, being seen in service still in 1964.

At Drogheda on the Dublin to Belfast main line class V 4-4-0 No 86 *Peregrine* arrives with a northbound express in 1955. Trains running non stop through Drogheda are subject to a severe speed restriction due to the curve through the station and to the viaduct over the Boyne valley.

[*R. Stieber*

GNR secondary passenger services were worked by a variety of 4-4-0s of the G. T. Clifford family. Among the largest of these were the Q class such as No 136 seen here at Adelaide, Belfast. The net on the tender forms part of the automatic tablet catching equipment used on the Portadown to Londonderry route.

The oldest and most numerous Clifford 4-4-0s surviving in 1956 were the PP class introduced in 1896. These worked freight and passenger trains on all the border routes and branches and had a very good turn of speed. No 71 was photographed at Londonderry.

The largest goods engines on the GNR were Glover's class SG3 0-6-0s. No 8 was photographed at Adelaide depot in 1956.

The class AL 0-6-0s dating from 1893 were among the oldest GNR freight locomotives to survive in recent years. They were designed by J. C. Park and No 57 is seen here at Londonderry.

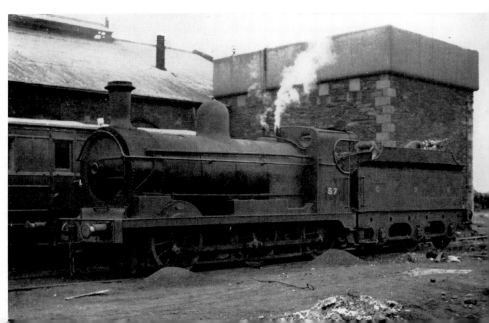

The last of the Clifford JT 2-4-2Ts were allocated to Clones depot and worked the short branch line between Ballyhaise and Belturbet. One of these has been preserved at the transport museum at Belfast.

The GN had relatively few freight tanks or shunting locomotives. 0-6-4Ts appear to have been favoured for the Belfast docks lines. Clifford class RT No 22 was seen pausing between movements near Ulster Transport's Queen's Quay station.

The few 0-6-2Ts were normally seen in the Dundalk or Dublin areas. They were smart looking engines, like No 99 here, of class QGTs, at Dundalk.
[*R. Stieber*

The Great Northern 'Enterprise'

The Great Northern's crack " Enterprise " train, non stop from Belfast to Dublin, approaches Dundalk, Eire, from the North. It is headed in this 1956 photograph by McIntosh three cylinder simple 4-4-0 No 209 *Foyle*. Twelve months after this July 1956 photograph was taken steam had been completely displaced from the " Enterprise " trains.

By 1956 the Dublin based " Enterprise " service had been dieselised. The train, here seen passing through Dundalk, comprised two AEC Park Royal 250 hp diesel mechanical railcars with two trailers (including a buffet) converted from locomotive hauled stock. The " Enterprise " buffet cars were unusual in that due to the differing excise duties on wines and spirits north and south of the Irish border each car had two separate drinks cabinets, one of which was stocked in Eire for use south of the border only and the other being stocked in Belfast and kept unlocked only north of the border!

In 1957 new 300 hp railcars were being erected at Dundalk Works and enabled the Belfast based " Enterprise " train to be modernised. In this 1957 photograph the eight coach train has two railcars at each end, all railcars having corridor connections throughout. These were intended to be intermediate railcars as when the last batch of single ended cars followed, the train had one of these at each end with an intermediate car coupled ' inside ' and presented a more complete appearance.

Class PP 4-4-0 No 42 arrives at Strabane with a stopping train from Omagh during a cloudburst (nothing unusual in those parts!). In the right foreground is the interesting turntable which could accommodate both 5ft 3in gauge and 3ft gauge locomotives.

The

Great

Northern

Border

Lines

The morning train from Londonderry to Belfast via Dungannon leaves Strabane behind class S2 4-4-0 No 191 *Croagh Patrick*, resplendent in blue livery.

In the last summer of Great Northern section services to Londonderry, 1964, class S 4-4-0 No 171 arrives alongside the River Foyle with the afternoon train from Belfast.
[*A. Trickett*

Enniskillen station with (left) a diesel railcar train for Clones and Belfast, and (right) Glover class U mixed traffic 4-4-0 No 197 on a stopping train from Dundalk to Bundoran.

Two PP 4-4-0s pull out of Enniskillen with a passenger train for Omagh in 1957.

Clones station, with, left to right, McKin-
tosh class U 4-4-0 No 205 *Down* with a
train for Cavan, diesel railcars for Armagh
and Belfast, and a PP 4-4-0 on a stopping
train to Dundalk.

Ballyhaise station with (left) a Cavan to
Clones train headed by PP 4-4-0 No 72
and (right) the connection from Belturbet
which has arrived behind 2-4-2T No 91.

The Great Northern Railway route between Enniskillen and Omagh passed the small town of Fintona at about $\frac{1}{2}$ mile distance. The short branch line from Fintona Junction was worked very economically to the end of its life (autumn 1957) by one horse and the famous tram, pictured here arriving at Fintona.   The tram was able to take three classes of passengers—third class on top, second class inside at the front (i.e. to windward of the horse), and first class inside at the back.   It is now preserved at the Belfast Transport Museum.

Two GNR 5ft 3in gauge electric trams at Hill of Howth station.   This tramway ran from Sutton and climbed the south side of the hill giving fine views across the entrance to Dublin harbour and to the hills beyond.   After the summit the route curved north-wards and dropped over the hill with further excellent views over Howth harbour with its fishing fleet.   Both at Sutton and at Howth the tramway connected with trains on the GNR Howth branch and made available a delightful evening excursion from the Dublin area.

Passenger services on the GNR line from Drogheda to Navan and Oldcastle were in later years worked by diesel railbuses such as No 2 illustrated here. The rear wheels on this car were pneumatic tyred with outer rims of steel, a system patented by G. B. Howden, a former Chief Mechanical Engineer of the GNR, and Meredith. On most of the railbuses all wheels were of this type.

The Dundalk Works shunting locomotive was this 1928 built Hawthorn Leslie 0-6-0T crane engine No 31. After the dissolution of the Great Northern Railway the works at Dundalk were taken over by Dealgan Industries who have developed there a thriving engineering concern producing, among other things, steel castings, equipment for the Irish Turf Board and commercial vehicles.

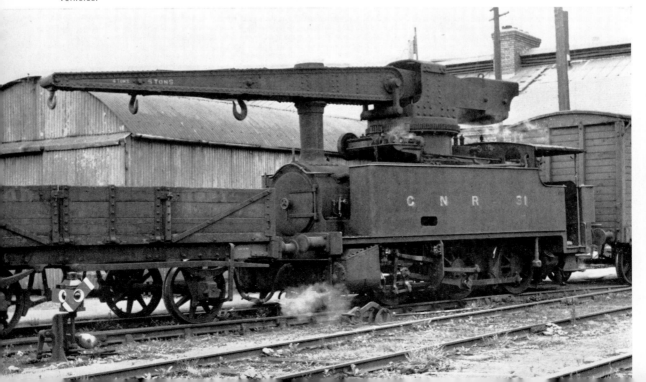

The nameplate and crest on U class locomotive No 203 *Armagh*. The Great
Northern Railway crest included the coats of arms of Ulster (in the centre), Belfast,
Dublin, Londonderry, Dundalk, and Enniskillen.

Apart from a few workings to and from Drogheda, the main Great Northern suburban activity in the Dublin area was confined to the Howth branch. Two pairs of Gardner engined articulated diesel railcars shared this traffic. One of them, railcar G, is pictured arriving at Amiens Street. They were the ultimate extension of the principle adopted on the Gardner-Walker narrow gauge cars, the engine unit being in the rigid section with the passenger portions articulated to either end of it. When CIE took over the GN section south of the border they integrated the Howth workings with the route to Bray and Greystones and the whole Dublin suburban service was revised and diagrammed for Park Royal railcars with higher density seating installed.

For its secondary line services stopping at wayside halts the Great Northern Railway also had small number of Gardner-Walker articulated railcars of the same basic type as the narrow gauge railways. One of these, No C1, is seen leaving Enniskillen towing its tiny luggage trailer.

Despite its early entry into the field of diesel railcars, the Great Northern Railway made practically no use of diesel locomotives. An exception was the M.a.K. 0-8-0 diesel mechanical 800 hp locomotive which was delivered early in the 1950s. This became part of CIE stock in 1958 and was photographed at Inchicore in 1963.

The Belfast firm of Harland and Wolff made a number of attempts to gain entry into the diesel locomotive market. In 1937 it delivered to the B&CDR for trials 500 hp Bo-Bo diesel electric locomotive No 28. This was moved to the NCC in 1944, and by 1956 was working on the Great Northern Railway at Adelaide where this photograph was taken.

After 1958 when UTA took over the Great Northern lines north of the border, considerable use was made of the WT class 2-6-4Ts on GN section suburban services to which they were well suited.   This 1964 photograph shows No 57 passing Adelaide on a southbound train.   After the closures of all other GN passenger routes enough diesel railcars were made available to take over all suburban services and steam had disappeared from the GN section by the author's last visit in 1967.   [A. Trickett

Belfast

Class S 4-4-0 No 174 *Carrantuohill* arrives at Portadown with a stopping train from Belfast.   [A. Trickett

By 1964 there was a shortage of steam power on the Great Northern section of UTA, which was subsequently relieved by the release of stock from the closure of the Portadown to Londonderry line.   During the time of the shortage even the sole surviving VS 4-4-0 No 207 *Boyne* was pressed into suburban work, as seen in this view of a stopping train leaving Belfast. ⌈*A. Trickett*

Suburban

Drifting into Adelaide station on a southbound working from Belfast is class S 4-4-0 No 60 *Slieve Donard* (ex GNR No 172). [*A. Trickett*

The Great Northern Railway (Ireland) had about twenty five 4-4-2Ts of classes T1 and T2 which included some Belfast suburban workings among their duties. This photograph shows T2 No 5X at Great Victoria Street station, Belfast, in UTA days.   [*A. Trickett*

The Modern Great Northern

Two views of class S2 4-4-0 *Lugnaquilla*. The upper photograph shows the engine in blue livery as GNR No 190. By 1963 when the lower photograph was taken at Londonderry *Lugnaquilla* had become part of the stock of Ulster Transport and had been painted in that Authority's black livery with yellow and red lining and the number 62.

GNR goods engines that were taken into UTA stock were renumbered into that concern's stock. These two photographs taken at Londonderry show (upper) class QLG No 109 in 1956, and (lower) class SG2 0-6-0 as UTA No 40 (previously GNR No 18), in 1963.

Those ex Great Northern Railway locomotives that the UTA planned to displace were not renumbered into UT stock but were given the suffix X after their GN numbers. One or two of them nevertheless remained in existence for many years, as witness the old Clifford class PG 0-6-0 No 10X seen at Belfast Adelaide depot as late as 1963.

While the excursion passengers from Belfast enjoy the delights of Dublin, their locomotive, 4-4-0 No 207 *Boyne,* is serviced at the CIE locomotive depot at Amiens Street.   It has strange company in the form of ex GS&WR J15 0-6-0 No 130, one of the last condemned locomotives standing on CIE tracks.

[*A. Trickett*

In 1964, over a year after steam working had ceased on CIE, excursions from Belfast to Dublin were worked throughout by steam traction, usually W class 2-6-0s, a VS 4-4-0 or even a WT 2-6-4T fitted with a separate water tender.   In this picture VS 4-4-0 No 207 *Boyne* arrives at Dublin Amiens Street with a train of ex GNR stock in UTA dark green livery.   The locomotive is still in ex Great Northern blue and carries its old GN number.   This is because at the time the GNR was divided No 207 became part of CIE stock, was not renumbered, and was sold to the UTA in 1963!

[*A. Trickett*

Day Excursion to the North

At the end of the day the Belfast excursion pulls steadily out of Dublin's Amiens Street station.   The sound of No 207's three cylinder beat was a rare experience for Dubliners by 1964.

[*A. Trickett*

Above: After taking over the GN lines south of the border CIE obtained further deliveries of General Motors Bo-Bo diesel electrics. Two of these, Nos B154 and B144, are pictured arriving at Drogheda with the 9.15 from Dublin to Belfast. The train is composed of some ex GNR stock in CIE light green livery at the front (for Dundalk) and modern CIE stock at the rear for Belfast, and was photographed in 1963.

Left: The 9.15 from Dublin to Belfast leaving Dundalk after changing engines from CIE diesels to ex NCC class WT 2-6-4T No 54. This type was transferred in part to the ex GN lines taken over by the UTA and heralded the withdrawal of the V class compounds whose duties they took over without difficulty north of Dundalk.

The Divided Main Line

A Belfast to Dublin through train pulls out of Great Victoria Street station, Belfast, behind a WT 2-6-4T. The train consists of GN type stock in UTA dark green livery.
[A. Trickett

With a southbound train of mixed CIE and UTA stock (all ex GNR) class WT 2-6-4T No 50 accelerates past Adelaide in the suburbs of Belfast. [A. Trickett

South of the border CIE continued to develop the ex GNR freight services, integrating them with the rest of the CIE network. In this view of the Boyne bridge at Drogheda, a 960 hp GM diesel electric locomotive hauls a goods train northwards up the old GNR main line.

Ex Great Northern Railway class S 4-4-0 No 171 on the turntable at Portadown motive power depot in June 1963. Although No 171 had stencilled 'CIE' on its buffer beam it had just been handed over to Ulster Transport who had purchased a number of ex GN locomotives to augment their fleet. No 171, which in Great Northern days carried the name *Slieve Gullion*, has recently been acquired by a preservation society and is stored in the old NCC depot at Whitehead.

In 1915 the Great Northern Railway (Ireland) introduced to the designs of GT Glover a small mixed traffic 4-4-0 type, class U (see page 73). A further five engines were added to the class by H. McIntosh in 1948, with detail differences. One of these, No 204 *Antrim*, was photographed at Dundalk in 1963. Being at that time in CIE stock it had retained its blue livery and GN number.

The Great Northern U Family

Those of the U class that had gone into Ulster Transport stock were soon painted black and renumbered. This photograph shows No 68 *Down* (old No 205) at Portadown.

Glover introduced in 1921 a tank version of his U class, designated class T2 4-4-2T, of which No 69 is pictured at Adelaide. An interesting feature of this type was the bogie brake.

The goods version of the U class was the UG 0-6-0 type. The photograph shows one as UTA No 47 in lined black livery at Adelaide in 1963.

The Modern 'Enterprise'

The 11.30 " Enterprise Express " non stop from Belfast to Dublin Connolly station crosses the Boyne bridge at Drogheda in October 1967 behind a General Motors Bo-Bo diesel electric locomotive.   This train set included two baggage cars, a train heating van, an ex Great Northern first class coach and three of the latest CIE vehicles, some with B4 type bogies as used on British Railways' latest stock.   This CIE train set was making two out-and-home journeys daily from Dublin.

The Northern Ireland Railways " Enterprise Express " set rounding the curves near Pointzpass on the ex Great Northern main line north of the border with Eire. The leading railcar is one of the last GNR 300 hp cars to be built at Dundalk, and the rear car is one of the intermediate type with corridor connections at both ends. The buffet and brake coach are ex locomotive hauled stock of GNR design. The train is painted in the red and cream style adopted by NIR in 1966. This four car unit worked two return " Enterprise " trains each day and in this view was forming the 2.30 from Belfast Great Victoria Street to Dublin Connolly calling at Portadown and Dundalk.

In October 1967 the 2.30 Belfast to Dublin " Enterprise Express " formed of a four car NIR (ex GNR) railcar set approaches the site of the old station at Goraghwood, at which in earlier years all passenger trains other than non stops called for customs examinations. The " Enterprise " trains in GNR days had customs examinations arranged at Belfast and Dublin terminals, but since the present service was introduced this activity takes place on the train, thus affording an effective improvement in overall journey time.

Ulster Transport

THE ULSTER TRANSPORT AUTHORITY railways had three main constituents, the ex LMS (Northern Counties Committee) lines north of Belfast, the Belfast and County Down Railway to the south east, and more recently those parts of the Great Northern Railway north of the border. The UTA in conjunction with the GNR also had control of the narrow gauge County Donegal Railways through a joint committee.

By 1956 the Belfast and County Down Railway had shrunk to one double track commuter railway from Belfast Queen's Quay station to Holywood and Bangor on the south side of Belfast Lough, and its neat 4-4-2Ts and powerful 4-6-4Ts had been broken up, with the exception of one 4-4-2T being restored for the Belfast Transport Museum. Diesel multiple units composed of some modern sliding door diesel hydraulic railcars, matching trailers, and some strengthening trailers of locomotive hauled non-corridor stock now run an efficient and economically sound service on this line.

Out of York Road station, north of Belfast's city centre, steam still reigned supreme in the late 1950s, apart from a few railcars running on the Larne line along that most attractive north shore of Belfast Lough. The Midland Railway of England had taken over the Belfast and Northern Counties Railway in 1903 and likewise the London, Midland and Scottish Railway inherited it in 1923, and its last steam locomotives were therefore largely of LMS or Midland designs. Very few of the U2 4-4-0s (similar to MR 3Ps) remained by 1957, though there were three 0-6-0s of distinct B&NCR outline but dating from 1923. However most main line trains were in the capable hands of class W 2-6-0s, impressive looking machines that were tender derivatives of Fowler's LMS 4P 2-6-4Ts but with 6ft wheels. Most freight and local passenger trains were handled by 2-6-4Ts of class WT, identical in most respects to the tender engines. These locomotives had been erected by the NCC in Belfast from parts made in Derby, and even as late as 1964 their heavy boiler repairs were being carried out by British Railways, mostly at Derby locomotive works though the last few were overhauled at Swindon.

The UTA painted its locomotives black, with yellow and red lining, and its passenger stock was a drab, dark green.

From Belfast the Londonderry main line climbs steeply past the junction with the Larne line, drops down to Antrim, and remains double tracked as far as Ballymena after which passing loops are laid out for high speed running. On the author's footplate trips on this line speeds of up to 70 mph were attained and automatic tablet catching dealt efficiently with 60 mph running through passing loops.

At Coleraine the Portrush branch leaves the main line which then curves westwards, passing beneath the cliffs of the north Londonderry coast, approaching the county town along the shores of Lough Foyle.

Modernisation of UTA has proceeded apace, the main line being dealt with in two stages. 275 hp diesel hydraulic railcars that could also haul freight at night were made up with trailers and restaurant cars to form 6-car trains of 1,100 hp capable of up to 90 mph. These railcars had been converted from existing locomotive hauled stock but were pleasant to ride in and enabled a very fast service to be run, including start to stop runs in even time over relatively short distances. These were displaced in 1966 by new 600 hp diesel electric railcars running with second hand trailers. The 600 hp engines were by English Electric to the same basic 4-SRKT design as in the diesel electric multiple units on the Southern Region of British Railways. These new trains are painted in the Northern Ireland Railways Co. livery of dark red and white.

After the nationalisation of the GNR in 1958, ex NCC steam locomotives ventured much farther afield, on to the Portadown-Londonderry line, and between Belfast and Dundalk. Even certain special trains from Belfast to Dublin had W 2-6-0s throughout, appearing for the first time in Eire's capital when that country's steam locomotives were practically gone! The UTA also began painting black those blue GNR locomotives which it inherited, though by 1963 this had stopped and they were even buying surplus GNR engines from CIE to bridge the period until 1966 when steam largely finished working! In 1967 only eight steam locomotives, WT 2-6-4Ts, and *Lough Erne* were in use on NIR on limited freight duties.

A new diesel electric multiple unit six car train of Northern Ireland Railways threads the tunnels between Castlerock and Downhill on the beautiful coastline of northern County Londonderry.   The train is the 8.35 from Belfast to Londonderry, running on a fast two hour schedule.   The headland in the background is actually part of County Donegal, Eire, and marks the entrance to Lough Foyle.

The last surviving Belfast and County Down steam locomotive was 4-4-2T No 30, pictured in York Road Works, Belfast, being restored for preservation in Belfast Transport Museum. No 30 was one of twelve 4-4-2Ts delivered by Beyer Peacock between 1901 and 1921 and were among the most successful locomotives on the B&CDR.

A flashback to steam days on the Belfast and County Down Railway. Beyer Peacock 4-4-2T No 18 pulls out of Newcastle with a train of six-wheelers for Belfast Queen's Quay.

[*The late J. F. Keenan*

In 1955, shortly after the Bangor line had been dieselised, the displaced steam locomotives from the B&CD section were standing in Belfast Queen's Quay depot awaiting disposal. This photograph shows from right to left class 6 2-4-0 No 206 (B&CD No 6), class 4 0-6-0 No 210 (B&CD No 4), two class 22 4-6-4Ts, and two 4-4-2Ts. Nearly all were built by Beyer Peacock. [R. Stieber

The lines of the British LM&SR 3P 4-4-0s are self-evident in this 1957 shot of ex Northern Counties Committee class U2 No 86. A number of this type had names of castles in the counties served by the NCC lines. They were employed mainly on passenger trains between Belfast and Londonderry, but were displaced from the fastest trains by class W 2-6-0s.

Ex Northern Counties Committee (LMS) 0-6-0 of class V, built 1923, at Belfast York Road depot. These were about the last locomotives to display signs of Belfast and Northern Counties Railway practice in their appearance, despite a very strong Midland Railway (Derby) influence in their design, and were still in service in 1957.

The handsome lines of the class W 2-6-0 tender engines are displayed here by No 91 *The Bush*, named after a small river in County Antrim. This photograph shows No 91 at Dublin in 1963 when it was working on the Great Northern section. It had worked an excursion non stop from Belfast earlier in the day.

In 1946 delivery began of kits of parts for the class WT 2-6-4Ts for erection in Belfast. These were built for the suburban trains to Larne and Ballymena and did general freight service also. This photograph shows No 1 at York Road, Belfast. Some of the latest batch, delivered about 1950, were later transferred to the Great Northern lines taken over by the Ulster Transport Authority and did some excellent work on the main line to Dundalk.

In 1944 two class 3F 0-6-0Ts were transferred from the LM&SR to the NCC, converted to 5ft 3in gauge, and set to work shunting at Belfast. Known as class Y, No 19 was seen at York Road in 1957.

Harland and Wolff diesel locomotives were brought into service on the NCC section of UTA in the form of shunting locomotives. The smallest, No 16, was photographed at York Road in 1956.

The Coast Road to Derry

With brakes hard on and steam blowing furiously from its safety valves, class W 2-6-0 No 94, with narrow tender, arrives at Ballymoney with a Belfast to Londonderry train in 1957.

On a train from Belfast to Londonderry, UTA class W 2-6-0 No 93 *The Foyle* arrives at Coleraine. The up to date nature of operations on this line are clear from the inclusion in this 1957 photograph of colour light signals.

By 1963 services on the UTA coast route to Londonderry had been running for a number of years at greatly improved speeds due to the introduction of these 275 hp Rolls-Royce engined diesel hydraulic railcars. Four of these cars with two trailers could make up a six car train with sufficient power to attain speeds up to 90 miles per hour. At night time when passenger trains were very few two of these cars coupled together could haul freight trains of moderate weight, which in view of the Northern Ireland government's policy of diverting most freight haulage to road adequately dealt with most of the freight traffic still remaining on rail. This multi-purpose feature was made possible by equipping the railcars with hydro-mechanical transmission consisting of a hydraulic torque convertor driving through a four-speed gearbox which changed automatically at the required speeds. This view shows three multi-purpose railcars hauling some non-passenger coaching stock on a slow working to Belfast about to leave Londonderry Waterside station.

Above: The latest diesel multiple units to work in Ireland are the diesel electric trains of Northern Ireland Railways. The 11.25 from Belfast (York Road) to Londonderry (Waterside) is seen leaving Coleraine in October 1967.

Below: The 11.15 from Londonderry to Belfast under the cliffs at Downhill. These trains were introduced in 1966 by Northern Ireland Railways. They are each powered by two diesel electric railcars, the mechanical parts of which were supplied by English Electric and bodies built at the UTA works at Duncrue Street, Belfast. Each car is powered by an EE 4SRKT 600 hp four cylinder power unit. The trailer coaches were converted by UTA from existing loco-motive hauled stock. On the introduction of these trains the multi-purpose diesel hydraulic cars were rediagrammed onto stopping services on the Londonderry and Larne lines, and brought steam operation of passenger trains to an almost complete end in Ireland.

A 1967 view along the beach at Downhill, County Londonderry, showing, dwarfed by the high cliffs as it passes Downhill station, the 11.15 diesel electric train from Londonderry to Belfast.

Tail view of the 11.15 from Londonderry to Belfast as it enters
the tunnels between Downhill and Castlerock, Northern Ireland
Railways.

Belfast
Suburban

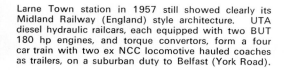

Larne Town station in 1957 still showed clearly its Midland Railway (England) style architecture. UTA diesel hydraulic railcars, each equipped with two BUT 180 hp engines, and torque convertors, form a four car train with two ex NCC locomotive hauled coaches as trailers, on a suburban duty to Belfast (York Road).

The remaining line of the old Belfast and County Down Railway is the Bangor branch. A frequent service of diesel railcar trains has proved to be the most profitable of Ulster Transport railway operations, and in this view of Bangor station a diesel train is preparing to return to Belfast (Queen's Quay).

Additional suburban diesel railcars working on the multi-purpose principle were produced in the late 1950s and early 1960s, converted from existing locomotive hauled stock. These were principally for the Larne route. A pair of multi-purpose suburban railcars is seen here arriving at York Road in 1963.

The nameplate of UTA class U2 4-4-0 No 75 *Antrim Castle*.   [*R. Stieber*

County Donegal Railways

IF ONE ALIGHTED from a GNR train at Strabane in the late 1950s and crossed to the island platform at the west of the station one would normally find two small 3ft gauge railcars of peculiar type pointing respectively towards the Letterkenny line and towards Stranorlar and Donegal.

Customs formalities always delayed one's eager attempts to gain a closer look at these and at the 4-6-4 or 2-6-4 tank locomotive just making up a freight train, but on closer inspection one would see that the railcars were articulated, the front bogie carrying engine and gearbox and driver's cab. On starting away from Strabane one would hear a strange jangling from the coupling rods echo back from the signal box. The Eire customs were met at Castlefin, and the railway would continue its straight, evenly graded course to Stranorlar on a track bed originally built for the broad gauge. Stranorlar was the administrative and maintenance centre of the CDRJC.

Beyond Stranorlar the line climbed south-westwards over the wild, barren highland, crossing the peak through Barnesmore Gap, and then running down past Lough Eske to Donegal. From this county town two branches departed, one southwards to Ballyshannon where it just failed to connect with the GNR Bundoran branch, and the other continuing westwards along the north shore of Donegal Bay to the little fishing port of Killybegs.

All regular passenger trains on all routes were operated by red and cream diesel railcars, varying in age from No 10 (ex Clougher Valley Railway) of the early 1930s to No 20 delivered in 1951. Both Nos 19 and 20 have since passed to the Isle of Man Railway. As the railcars on the CDR were unidirectional they were turned on locomotive turntables at each terminus.

The author well recalls a journey made in 1957 which illustrates Donegal train working in recent years. Leaving Killybegs, railcar 20 had one bogie saloon coach and a van in tow. At Donegal, railcar No 12 was cut in behind No 20, and one more coach and a further van added. This cavalcade, each railcar with its own driver, began the climb to Barnesmore Gap in fine style until about half way up when the second railcar's radiator began to boil over! For the rest of the climb, the view out of the rear windows of No 20 was blocked by sprays of steam and water which from a distance must have been impressive to view. At Stranorlar one of the corridor bogie coaches transferred from the NCC's defunct narrow gauge Ballymena to Larne boat service was inserted in the train, which then ran to Strabane as—railcars 20 and 12 hauling three coaches and two vans, seven vehicles in all.

Normally, trains of such length were infrequent but on many Sundays excursions were run from Strabane to Rossnowlagh on the east shore of Donegal Bay, and these were one duty of the line's lovely steam locomotives. Up to 1956 these superheated 2-6-4Ts (and two 4-6-4Ts) were painted geranium red and kept very smart indeed. In 1957 the author noted that a darker shade of red was in use. The locomotives were normally engaged on freight work, of which there was plenty, all vacuum braked and all with red-and-cream passenger brake vans at the tail!

An oddity was the solitary diesel shunter No 11 *Phœnix*. This was acquired from the Clougher Valley Railway in 1932 and was rebuilt with a Gardner 6L2 engine of the same type as that used in the railcars.

After the line's closure on 1st January 1960 interest in the County Donegal Railways came from an unexpected quarter. An American purchased two 2-6-4T locomotives (*Meenglas* and *Drumboe*), some rolling stock and a large quantity of track. These were stored at Strabane station at the time the author last saw them in 1963 prior to their despatch to the United States. How soon part of the County Donegal Railways (Ireland's last narrow gauge system) will be reborn across the ocean only time can tell.

Diesel railcar No 15 of the County Donegal Railways approaches Ballyshannon from Donegal. This delightful railway system was jointly owned by the Ulster Transport Authority and the Great Northern Railway and provided an adequate service in a county that was, to say the least, somewhat sparsely populated.

The freight trains on the CDR were worked by attractive cherry red steam locomotives of powerful 4-6-4T or 2-6-4T type. No 5 *Drumboe*, seen here at Stranorlar in 1956, was one of a class supplied by Nasmyth Wilson in 1907 and 1908. The CDR steam locomotives were the only superheated narrow gauge engines in Ireland.

One of the larger County Donegal railcars, No 15 photographed at Ballyshannon in 1957. The coupling rods by which the power bogie wheels were coupled are clearly visible beneath the cab.

Station scene at Donegal with, on the left, two railcars on a service to Strabane, on the right railcar 20 and trailer destined for Killybegs, and steam locomotive No. 6 *Columbkille* shunting in the background. Railcar 20, the latest of a line of articulated cars built by Walker of Wigan, is now part of the stock of the Isle of Man Railway.

At the fishing village of Killybegs, railcar 20 is shunting stock to make up the 1 pm to Donegal and Strabane.

A pleasant scene at Castlefin on the Finn Valley line between Stranorlar and Strabane, as 2-6-4T No 6 *Columbkille* enters the station with a freight. The Finn Valley Railway was originally built to 5ft 3in gauge but was converted to 3ft gauge in 1894 to link with the existing narrow gauge line from Stranorlar to Donegal.

The firm of Walker Bros. of Wigan, Lancashire, built the majority of Ireland's light railcars. They were of unusual design having a rigid driving bogie carrying the cab, Gardner diesel engine and transmission, with the passenger portion articulated to the leading bogie. One of the earliest was County Donegal Railways No 10, originally purchased from the Clougher Valley Railway, seen here at Stranorlar in 1956.

The ex Clougher Valley Railway steam tractor, rebuilt as County Donegal Railways diesel locomotive No 11 *Phoenix*, photographed at Strabane in 1957.

After the closure of the County Donegal Railways in 1960 the two latest railcars (1951 built) were sold to the Isle of Man Railway. They are seen in this scene with No 20 towing No 19 on a Douglas to Peel working in 1962, passing Beyer Peacock 2-4-0T No 5 *Mona* at St. Johns.

County Donegal Railways class 5 2-6-4T No 4 *Meenglas* takes water in the locomotive yard at Stranorlar.   [*R. Stieber*

The Sligo, Leitrim and Northern Counties Railway

LEAVING THE Northern town of Enniskillen on the Great Northern route from Dundalk to Omagh, a single 5ft 3in gauge track ran westwards into Eire, across much poor countryside, and joined the CIE line from the south to Sligo about five miles short of that port. The SL&NCR was, in 1956, the shortest railway in Ireland (43¼ miles long from end to end). It was the only independent railway still in existence in the 1950s that crossed the border between Northern Ireland and Eire, probably because neither government chose to nationalise it, though the government of Eire did give it a sizeable annual grant that kept it running until 1957. In that year the GN line through Enniskillen was closed and so the outlet of the SL&NCR's through cattle traffic (its main raison d'être in recent years) disappeared, precipitating its immediate closure.

To the railway enthusiast the SL&NCR was unique. Through most of its life it ran its locomotive hauled trains only with tank engines and these were of one type, Beyer Peacock long-boilered 0-6-4Ts, though three successively improved groups of these were put into service from 1882 to 1951. Its locomotives were not numbered, being identified by names only. The last two, delivered to the railway in 1951, were never owned by the SL&NCR. The credit purchase arrangements with the manufacturers were not concluded, and Beyer Peacock affixed plates to their bunkers affirming their ownership of both *Lough Erne* and *Lough Melvin*. These two were purchased by the Ulster Transport Authority when the SL&NCR closed, and ended their days on the Belfast dock lines.

In recent years passenger services between Enniskillen and Sligo were with one exception worked by a Gardner-Walker articulated railcar, known as railcar B, and by two railbuses converted from road buses by fitting Howden-Meredith type wheels with steel rims encasing pneumatic tyres. These were maintained in an attractive livery of two tone green with white roofs. The one survivor of these is railcar B which was purchased by CIE, painted black, gold and white and numbered 2509, and set to work between Limerick and Nenagh.

The one passenger train that was the exception to the "railcars only" rule was the 7.30 pm mixed train from Enniskillen to Sligo. On the author's first visit to the SL&NCR this train was composed of 0-6-4T *Sir Henry* of the intermediate batch, a tri-composite brake coach, and a string of empty cattle trucks and a brake van. *Sir Henry* sported a Great Northern style chimney, presumably obtained during overhaul at the GNR works at Dundalk. The passenger coach was an oddity, being of clerestory style although built in the 1920s, and was the line's only bogie coach. On the author's journey *Sir Henry* showed a good turn of speed and was very smooth riding. Customs examinations at Glenfarne and Belcoo were brief. During the stop for water at Manorhamilton, where the railway's workshops were, photographs were taken of one of the two surviving Leitrim class 0-6-4Ts, *Lissadell* which was by then derelict. Its sister engine *Hazlewood* was still in use up to the line's closure in 1957.

After the train had detached its cattle wagons at Collooney, and the CIE line had been joined at Ballysodare, *Sir Henry* finished his run in fine style with a sprint at 60 miles per hour past the mountain sporting Queen Maeve's grave, to arrive at the glass roofed fortress that is Sligo station.

Above: The Killyhevlin viaduct, or Weir's Bridge, just beyond Enniskillen station on the SL&NCR. This was the only major civil engineering feature on the railway which otherwise had been built with a minimum of expense. Cutting and embankment sides were generally very steep so as to keep the purchase of land to a minimum during construction, but this tended later to result in a high rate of bank slippage.

Left upper: With steam leaking from every joint and the track bending under its weight, Beyer Peacock 0-6-4T *Lough Erne* eases the 11.00 am freight from Sligo to Enniskillen into Belcoo station. [*R. Stieber*

Left lower: The 7.20 pm mixed train from Enniskillen to Sligo standing at Belcoo, Eire, during the stop for customs examination. The locomotive is Beyer Peacock 0-6-4T *Sir Henry*, the first of three built between 1904 and 1917, an enlargement of the original '*Leitrim*' class. The photograph, taken in August 1956, shows the unique tri-composite brake clerestory coach which was worked daily from Sligo on the morning freight train so as to be at Enniskillen in time for the 7.20.

One of the two diesel railbuses standing in the small locomotive shed at Enniskillen. This view shows one of the small trailers used for conveyance of luggage for which other space did not exist on the railbuses.

[R. Stieber

In recent years the passenger services on the SL&NCR were worked mainly by railbuses and this railcar, known as railcar B. In this view it is seen arriving at Enniskillen on an afternoon train from Sligo in 1956.

Beyer Peacock 0-6-4T *Lissadell* standing derelict at Manorhamilton in summer 1957. This was one of five locomotives of the 'Leitrim' class built between 1882 and 1899, which design formed the basis of most later engines delivered to this small railway.

Above left: The last 'Leitrim' 0-6-4T to remain in regular service was *Hazlewood*. In this 1957 photograph it is in the small locomotive workshop at Manorhamilton.

Above right: Sligo, Leitrim and Northern Counties Railway railcar B, photographed during a stop at Belcoo for customs examination. This car was unique among the Garner-Walker single unit vehicles in that it could be driven from either end and did not have to be turned after each journey.

Left: Lough Erne, one of two 0-6-4Ts delivered in 1951, pauses for water at Manorhamilton while working the 2 pm freight from Enniskillen to Sligo. This locomotive, and its sister *Lough Melvin*, were never owned by the Sligo, Leitrim and Northern Counties Railway and had small plates attached to their bunkers stating that the owners were Messrs. Beyer Peacock, the builders.

When the SL&NCR was closed in 1957 its physical assets were put up for auction. Railcar B was purchased by CIE and was put to work between Limerick and Nenagh. In its new guise as No 2509 in black, gold and white livery it is seen here at Birdhill.

When the Sligo, Leitrim and Northern Counties Railway closed in 1957 the two 'Lough' class engines were purchased by Ulster Transport. *Lough Melvin* went to Belfast Adelaide depot to replace a GNR RT 0-6-4T, and *Lough Erne* was allocated to York Road where it is seen in this 1963 photograph, bearing the UTA number 27.

Guinness Brewery Railways

At their St. James's Gate Brewery in Dublin, Messrs. Arthur Guinness used to run a most unique railway system which was still virtually in full operation in 1956. The railway linked the main sections of the brewery, which is on three levels, with the exchange sidings and also with a small quay on the River Liffey.

The greatest part of it was 1ft 10 in gauge, worked mainly by a fleet of tiny Planet 37 hp diesel locomotives. Their overall size was limited by the dimensions of the spiral tunnel which, with $2\frac{1}{2}$ complete turns at 1 in 39, linked the two main levels of the brewery. These diesel locomotives had largely displaced the strange little steam locomotives of which only five were extant at the time of the author's visit. These were very unique machines, however. They were specially designed by Irish engineer Samuel Geoghegan and built at the Cork Street Foundry, Dublin. This design had two cylinders placed above the boiler barrel driving an intermediate crankshaft from which vertical rods passed down the sides of the locomotive to drive the road wheels. The boiler barrel, including the firebox, was cylindrical.

The strangest feature of these unique machines was the ingenious way they could be converted quickly for broad gauge use. Geoghegan designed a haulage wagon of which at least three were built. It was so simple as to be the mark of genius. Each wagon consisted of a frame with four broad gauge road wheels, with a space inside it exactly matching the outline of a narrow gauge locomotive. When wanted for broad gauge working a small locomotive would be lowered into a haulage wagon, its wheels would rest on the driven wheels inside the wagon which would drive the road wheels through gearing.

Guinness also had three broad gauge locomotives, two steam and one diesel, which shunted the exchanged sidings and took loaded wagons to the CIE yard at Kingsbridge. Export orders were until recently shipped on to steam barges for the run down the Liffey to the docks. This work is now dealt with by road, the railway operations are therefore much reduced, and the Geoghegan steam locomotives are gone.

At least two of the narrow gauge engines have been preserved however, one at Towyn in Wales and one at the Belfast Transport Museum.

A 1ft 10in gauge Geoghegan 0-4-0T locomotive at the locomotive depot at St. James's Gate brewery, Dublin. This view of No 22 shows the position of the two cylinders attached above the boiler to the two very deep side frames. The end of the intermediate crankshaft and the vertical rod drive to the wheels can also be seen. The side tanks were outside the main frames. No 22 was built in 1912 by Wm. Spence & Son at their Cork Street Foundry, Dublin.

The rear view of Geoghegan locomotive No 22 at the Guinness Brewery, Dublin, showing the cylindrical firebox, the boiler mountings on their separate stand over the firebox, and the unusual arrangement of the axleboxes. Five of these locomotives were still in irregular use in 1956.

1ft 10in gauge steam locomotive No 21 standing in 5ft 3in gauge haulage wagon No 4. It was acting as standby for the three broad gauge shunting locomotives.

125

This view of the interior of a haulage wagon shows clearly the narrow gauge driven wheels, the gearcases enclosing the gearing for the drive to the broad gauge axles, and the broad gauge wheels of the wagon. The shape of the wagon was designed so that a locomotive could be lowered into it directly and then be immediately available for use without any bolting up being necessary.

The narrow gauge steam locomotives have been displaced by small 37 hp Planet diesel locomotives supplied by F. C. Hibberd & Co. This photograph shows No 32 by the cask sheds. The diesel locomotives were painted in Guinness's standard shade of dark blue. One of these machines was exhibited in London at the Festival of Britain exhibition in 1951.

One of the two Hudswell Clarke 0-4-0STs which were employed in the exchange sidings at St. James's Gate. The wheels and cylinders were encased to permit the locomotives to work safely through the public roads to Kingsbridge CIE with broad gauge rail traffic, though this duty has since become the province of diesel locomotive No 4.

Hudswell Clarke diesel locomotive No 4 approaching the brewery with a load of wagons from the CIE yard at Kingsbridge. This machine is one of Hudswell's 'Enterprise' series with the constant horsepower feature and mechanical transmission.

Until the late 1950s export Guinness used to leave the St. James's Gate brewery through a small quay on the south side of the River Liffey and be taken by small steam barges to the Dublin Docks. In this picture the barge *Sandyford* is approaching the centre of Dublin on the Liffey on a morning loaded trip.

128